Advanced Brief Strategic Therapy for Young People with Anorexia Nervosa

This important new book details a strategic and systemic model for short-term therapy with adolescent sufferers of anorexia nervosa, a psychopathology that seduces patients into starvation as doctors and family look on with increasing desperation. Supported by the successful treatment of hundreds of cases over the past 30 years, the book is the culmination of a long-term intervention programme developed at the Strategic Therapy Centre of Arezzo, Italy.

It begins by outlining the range of different eating disorders, before identifying the specific characteristics that adolescents with anorexia present. The variations of the pathology are then discussed. Not all patients present with the same symptoms; some sufferers over-exercise while others binge eat or self-harm. Substance abuse is also common, either with diuretics or chemicals; others self-induce *vomiting*. The therapeutic strategy will, of course, differ for each patient. Accessibly written throughout, the book concludes with two cases studies – complete with full transcripts – which illustrate the therapeutic process that allowed the patient to change their patterns of thinking, and the accompanying behaviours.

An insightful and invaluable work on this vital topic, the book will be essential reading for any professional working with adolescents presenting with anorexia, as well as the families of sufferers.

Giorgio Nardone is a Professor of Psychology of Change at the Link University in Rome, Italy. He is currently involved in research, training, and therapy at *Centro di Terapia Strategica of Arezzo*.

Elisa Valteroni is a psychotherapist and Associate Researcher at *Centro di Terapia Strategica of Arezzo*.

"This book is a groundbreaking manual for understanding and treating what many consider to be the most complex, treatment-resistant, and deadly of the mental health disorders. Nardone and Valteroni breakdown the varying types of anorexia and then provide innovative and evidence-based strategies for intervening with each of these types. This is a must read for any therapist working with adolescents and emerging adults with anorexia."

—Jeffrey B. Jackson, PhD Virginia Tech, United State of America

"In a book called "Advanced brief strategic therapy for young people with anorexia nervosa" Giorgio Nardone, one of the best known representatives of the strategic approach, and Elisa Valteroni indicates ways of treatment for different types of anorexia and present to the reader two transcriptions of therapy. This book offers valuable advice to any clinician confronted with the difficult problem of anorexia nervosa."

—Mony Elkaim. M. D, honorary professor, Free University of Brussels

"Based on their experience with hundreds of adolescent anorexia nervosa patients, Giorgio Nardone and Elisa Valteroni have written a unique and original therapeutic book for the treatment of anorexia nervosa in young women combining a brief strategic and systemic approach. The book offers new and provocative ideas that will certainly both stimulate and inspire all mental health workers in treating more effectively anorexia nervosa in young women and men."

—Dr Johan Vanderlinden Coordinator Eating Disorder Unit University Psychiatric Center KULeuven, Belgium, Research Fellow Faculty of Psychology and Pedagogy, Catholic University of Leuven

"Giorgio Nardone proves to be the navigated captain that knows the route of his ship and all the traps hidden beneath the waves of the complex varieties of Anorectic behavior. He charts a clear and tailored route in order to free patients and families by their emotional storms and teaches them how to safely reach the coast. The book offers a unique orientation map for facing and mastering the scaring Anorexia ocean."

—Prof. Camillo Loriedo Università di Roma "Sapienza"

Advanced Brief Strategic Therapy for Young People with Anorexia Nervosa

An Effective Guide for Clinicians

Giorgio Nardone and Elisa Valteroni

LONDON AND NEW YORK

© 2017 Adriano Salani Editore s.u.r.l. – Milano
Gruppo editoriale Mauri Spagnol
L'anoressia giovanile: una terapia efficace ed efficiente per i disturbi alimentary
Milano: Ponte alle Grazie
published by Ponte alle Grazie imprint)
by Giorgio Nardone, Elisa Valteroni
English edition
Translated by Michele Salvagno
Editing and proofreading: Jennifer Mark and Jeffrey B. Jackson

First published in English 2020
by Routledge
2 Park Square, Milton Park, Abingdon, Oxon, OX14 4RN

and by Routledge
52 Vanderbilt Avenue, New York, NY 10017

Routledge is an imprint of the Taylor & Francis Group, an informa business

© 2020 Taylor & Francis

The right of Giorgio Nardone and Elisa Valteroni to be identified as authors of this work has been asserted by them in accordance with sections 77 and 78 of the Copyright, Designs and Patents Act 1988.

All rights reserved. No part of this book may be reprinted or reproduced or utilised in any form or by any electronic, mechanical, or other means, now known or hereafter invented, including photocopying and recording, or in any information storage or retrieval system, without permission in writing from the publishers.

Trademark notice: Product or corporate names may be trademarks or registered trademarks, and are used only for identification and explanation without intent to infringe.

Library of Congress Cataloging-in-Publication Data
A catalog record for this title has been requested

ISBN: 978-0-367-46787-6 (hbk)
ISBN: 978-0-367-46788-3 (pbk)
ISBN: 978-1-003-03106-2 (ebk)

Typeset in Bembo
by Swales & Willis, Exeter, Devon, UK

Contents

1 **The most terrible and beloved psychopathology**   1

2 **Research-intervention on anorexia**   5
   Therapeutic factors 9

3 **Understanding the disorder**   13
   Pure juvenile anorexia 13
   Juvenile anorexia with exercising 15
   Juvenile anorexia with binge eating 16
   Juvenile anorexia with vomiting 16
   Juvenile anorexia with self-harming 18
   Juvenile anorexia with elimination 18
   Juvenile anorexia with substance abuse 19
   Polysymptomatic juvenile anorexia and/or borderline personality disorder 20

4 **Therapeutic treatment**   23
   Breaking the patterns of juvenile anorexia 23
   Juvenile anorexia with exercising: *therapeutic treatment* 30
   Juvenile anorexia with binge eating: *the treatment* 32
   Juvenile anorexia with vomiting: *the treatment* 34
   Juvenile anorexia with self-harming: *the treatment* 37
   Juvenile anorexia with elimination: *the treatment* 38
   Juvenile anorexia with substance abuse: *the treatment* 39
   Multi-symptomatic juvenile anorexia and/or borderline personality disorder: the treatment 39
   The treatment of juvenile anorexia: summarise to redefine 41

5	**Juvenile anorexia: the effective therapy: Giorgio Nardone, Elisa Valteroni, Gianluca Castelnuovo**	**44**

Introduction 44
Effectiveness and efficiency of the brief strategic therapy at the Strategic Therapy Centre (STC) in Arezzo 46

Appendix	49
Case 1 49	
Case 2 72	
Bibliography	100
Index	105

Chapter 1

The most terrible and beloved psychopathology

In the vast panorama of psychopathologies, only one has death as a direct consequence — anorexia. According to the World Health Organization, after road accidents, anorexia represents the second major cause of death in youth. It is the fear of every parent and the pathology most feared by psychotherapists, psychologists, and psychiatrists. It is estimated that, today, between 5% and 18% of cases still have fatal outcomes (American Psychiatric Association [APA], 2013; Casiero & Frishman, 2006; Fichter et al., 2008; Nielsen et al., 1998; Steinhausen, 2002; Steinhausen et al., 2003). Certainly, these are not reassuring figures, especially if one reflects on the fact that they have remained stable for a few decades. This means that, despite the progress in research, therapies for this mental health disorder still, in most cases, have little effect and often do not limit or reverse its dangerous progression.

As we will see in detail in the following pages, sometimes it is the therapeutic treatment itself that aggravates, rather than ameliorates, the disorder (Dalle Grave, 2015; Nardone & Selekman, 2011; Nardone et al., 2005; Steinhausen, 2006). Other disheartening data concern therapy effectiveness, which is measured at an international level by the National Association of Anorexia Nervosa and Associated Disorders (ANAD): only 40% of treatments have positive outcomes; 45% of cases become chronic; and the remaining 15% are, as previously mentioned, fatal. However, there is also a ray of hope. Certain therapeutic approaches are the exception, guaranteeing far higher healing rates which, in some cases, are double than general average. This book aims to describe and explain a therapeutic approach or treatment protocol in such a way as to be accessible to the general public.

One of the most surprising elements one can come across when entering the world of anorexia is the fact that, contrary to what common sense would suggest, it is precisely those who are or may become victims who do not fear this dangerous disease. This is because anorexia is the most "beloved" of all pathologies and is often embraced as a virtue instead of as a disorder.

To verify the truthfulness of this seemingly incredible statement, one need only enter the online discussion groups related to "ANA", as anorexia is affectionately referred to by its devotees, and one finds oneself immersed in a world of upsetting absurdity. Adolescent girls express their deep love for their pathology – which represents to them a state of grace and elevation – and exchange information on the sublime sensations induced by their condition. After all, abstinence from food and pleasure has always, and in all cultures, been considered a way to reach religious or esoteric ecstasy.

It is vital to understand that the human body, in the early stages of severely restricted food intake and consequent weight loss, undergoes biological changes involving the central nervous system, including an increase in the production of endorphins. These changes evoke a state of well-being and excitement comparable to that which results from the use of cocaine. This should suffice to explain the subtle and seductive nature of this pathology, which is likely to evolve, as in about two thirds of cases, into its worst variant: eating and *vomiting* to remain underweight or to lose weight. These actions then turn into the irrepressible compulsion to eat to vomit as a form of extreme pleasure (Nardone et al., 2005). In fact, adolescent girls speak of anorexia as a "passionate secret lover", a "pampering refuge", a "wonderful travel companion". Therefore, this seemingly paradoxical devotion to the most dangerous of mental pathologies should not surprise.

Moreover, we must also consider the non-trivial role played by social desirability in a disease that has always afflicted princesses, actresses, and other women who present models for young women to emulate. In recent decades, this element has become even more important due to the influence exerted by fashion on youth. It is apparent to all that the models who walk the runways and whose pictures fill fashion magazines represent an anorexic ideal of beauty. In the 1980s, top models presented a toned and sometimes even athletic body image. Since the mid-1990s, however, this image has seen a change from athletic to emaciated. In most cases, today's models are severely underweight and often suffer from eating disorders.

To no avail, some European States, concerned by the phenomenon and its impact on the health of young people, have required stylists to avoid using models who are too thin and below certain sizes during runway shows. Unfortunately, many stylists responded by restricting the dimensions of the size samples to circumvent these demands, which is why today's clothing sizes are smaller than those adopted in the 1990s.

In this regard, the words of the late sociologist Sabino Acquaviva come to mind. Although his words might sound provocative, he was a careful observer of the evolution of fashion. He warned of the "wicked pact" made by stylists with the directors of fashion magazines, who proposed an increasingly youthful, even adolescent, model of male beauty and an increasingly androgynous model of female beauty, in order to exalt a *unisex* ideal.

If we analyse the latest images in fashion advertisements and the physical characteristics of those who walk the runway, we certainly cannot argue with Sabino Acquaviva. Nonetheless, perhaps it is too much to blame the exponential increase of eating disorders in recent years on the fashion world.

In any case, the search for culprits does not help us find solutions. Instead, it only leads to moralistic condemnation. Fashion informs behaviours but, in turn, it is influenced by social customs. There is a reciprocal and circular influence between what is proposed as a new aesthetic reference point and what emerges from the mutations of habits and social styles. Undoubtedly, the publicity of a certain model aesthetic cannot be irrelevant or harmless for teenagers facing the reality of adolescent interpersonal relationships in which "looking the part" plays an important reassuring role.

An indirect influence on the onset of anorexia is provided by the high degree of well-being and sheer opulence of the food available to us today. In fact, throughout the course of history, cases of this psychopathology have only been found amongst the noble and wealthy; no starving person has ever fallen ill with anorexia. In this regard, an experience of mine from 1993 is emblematic. An Indian colleague who I had known during my studies in Palo Alto, and who had then gone on to become the director of a psychiatric hospital in Mumbai, came to visit me in Italy. She came to keep herself up to date on phobic and obsessive disorders, and she was surprised that I was also dealing with so many cases of anorexia because in India, at that time, there were very few cases and those only among the nobility. Thus, she had not considered anorexia to be a clinical issue of sufficient importance to justify a specific research-intervention project. Eleven years later, when India had attained greater average prosperity, my colleague returned to Italy to study the short-term treatment of the anorexic disorder and its variants as an epidemic of anorexia had now exploded in her country.

By virtue of these reflections, one can understand the paradox of anorexia, a phenomenon that frightens as much as it attracts, and a severe disease that is mistaken for an aspirational and sublime virtue.

However, we may add yet another paradox, one that is perhaps no less surprising to the layperson: the fact that public information campaigns on anorexia seem to increase rather than reduce the occurrence of the phenomenon; in other words, the more one talks about anorexia, the more it seems to grow. One need only think of how many television programmes, talk shows, and youth information programmes are dedicated to this theme, guaranteeing high ratings to a detrimental epidemiological effect.

We may recall the extreme case of Rome's administration, which commissioned a famous photographer to create an awareness campaign on anorexia. Huge posters were displayed throughout the city, showing a young skin-and-bones anorexic woman posing as a model. The aim was to shock and to thereby lower the incidence of extreme weight loss amongst the general public. However, these posters had the opposite effect. The campaign was instead widely viewed as a great advertisement for the beauty of being skinny, escalating to the point in which the initiative was enthusiastically greeted by numerous websites and social forums for anorexia. The young woman on the poster died shortly afterwards, as a result of the devastating effects of the very illness which had been inadvertently celebrated. Stories like this do not mean that we must be silent on the subject, but rather that we must treat it with attention and competence, avoiding advertising in ways that makes anorexia appear even more desirable than it already is.

Anorexia has the potential to spread even more aggressively than the *Werther effect*, namely the chain of emulative suicides carried out by young romantics upon reading the famous Goethe novel. In fact, adolescent girls entering into the world of adult relationships become easy prey for pervasive suggestions, as they are already distressed by the physiological changes of their bodies and by the emotional and cognitive changes that are characteristic at this age.

Chapter 2

Research-intervention on anorexia

In 1993, our research project for the development of an advanced therapeutic model for eating disorders began. In fact, our previous experience treating phobic and obsessive disorders (Nardone, 1996; Nardone & Watzlawick, 1993) produced such important outcomes that we were persuaded to tackle the challenge of devising treatments specifically for eating disorders.

The systemic and strategic approach to psychotherapy already had a tradition concerning the treatment of anorexia (Elkaim, 1995; Haley, 1973; Minuchin et al., 2009; Minuchin et al., 1975; Selvini Palazzoli, 1963). However, it became immediately and startlingly apparent that eating disorders had evolved considerably and were clearly differentiated from the typologies observed in previous decades. Previous reviews of the scientific literature and information from other relevant fields, conducted by numerous authors representing different theoretical paradigms of psychotherapy and psychiatry, appeared discordant and, above all, ineffective when compared to the results of therapies. These discrepancies were so unsatisfactory as to suggest that it was necessary to look at our research-intervention from a different perspective to those adopted by our colleagues who had preceded us.

It was a matter of reformulating the diagnostic observations, in addition to the therapeutic strategies, in the light of empirical observations resulting from direct clinical experience. In the 1990s, the criteria for diagnosing eating disorders included only two distinct clinical classifications: anorexia nervosa and bulimia nervosa. Although they included some subtypes, these classifications did not describe clinical types strongly characterised by a series of symptomatic behaviours such as *purging*, *exercising*, self-induced *vomiting*, and the succession of periods of restricted eating and *binge eating*. In our work, these behaviours appeared much more frequently than the two pathologies referred to in the *Diagnostic and Statistical Manual of Mental Disorders* (DSM), which at the time was in its fourth edition.[1]

In other words, the official criteria that were necessary to establish a diagnosis did not account for the factual realities highlighted by direct clinical observation. Therefore, the numerous variants of eating disorder were being forced into two opposing categories: on the one hand, food restriction as a symptom; on the other, excessive food consumption.

The first experimental empirical study conducted on 192 cases (Nardone et al., 2005) revealed that the majority of those patients who were diagnosed with anorexia ate and vomited several times a day. Among those who were diagnosed with bulimia, many alternated between periods of restricted eating and periods of *binge eating*.

It emerged that what had been considered a secondary symptom had actually become a disorder of its own, based on a peculiar form of pathological equilibrium. The hypothesis of an evolution of eating disorders in distinct pathological frameworks was corroborated by the fact that they required totally different therapeutic strategies from those applied up to that point for the treatment of anorexia and bulimia. This clearly indicated that the functioning of the pathology, in its formation and persistence, was quite different from that of the two original eating disorder classifications.

This empirical finding, according to which "it is the solution that has proven effective in *solving* the problem that *explains* the inner workings of the problem itself" (Nardone, 1997, 1998, 2003, 2009; Nardone & Portelli, 2005; Nardone & Watzlawick, 2005), allowed us to obtain two important results: one at the level of actual knowledge of the evolution of eating pathologies, the other at the level of the formulation of innovative therapeutic techniques, capable of sending these disorders into remission.

With regards to the first result, our work has led to the precise and rigorous formulation of the variants of anorexia, offering for the first time in the literature the description of the *vomiting* syndrome – which is still today improperly defined in psychiatric textbooks as anorexia nervosa with binging and purging, or as bulimia nervosa with purging – and *binge eating* disorder, which, has finally found space among the diagnostic criteria of the DSM-5 as a recognised and independent classification.

Therapeutic innovations for the treatment of eating disorders were developed through rigorous clinical trials and have now been empirically validated (Ball & Mitchell, 2004; Dare & Eisler, 1997; Le Grange, 2004; Le Grange et al., 2010; Lock et al., 2010; NCCMH, 2004; Robin et al., 1994, 1999; Russell et al., 1987; Vanderlinden, 2001) and are also used within therapy methods that differ from those proposed in this book.

In 1999, it was very touching to receive a letter from one of the masters of systemic and family therapy, a great expert in the treatment of anorexia, Dr. Mony Elkaim. He thanked me for my work on eating disorders that had shone light on a number of controversial issues that had hindered the development of a suitable and effective therapy. For this reason, Dr. Elkaim volunteered to curate the French edition of *Prisons of Food*, in which our research-intervention and its results were presented.

With regards to restrictive anorexia, the most important innovation concerning the treatment was the modification of the typical *diktat* of therapies practised up until that point. That is, the prohibition of talking about food and about the direct problems experienced by patients. These subjects were prohibited on the untested premise that discussing them was counter-productive.[2] During our experimentation, however, it became immediately apparent that treating the perceptions and reactions of people with anorexia in relation to food, their ambivalence between desire and fear, and in their emotional impact between inhibition and outburst represented a fundamental therapeutic step. Both the denied desire of the pleasure of eating forbidden foods and the associated fear of losing control of this restrictive behaviour proved to be actual targets for the therapy.

With this perspective, we began to test therapeutic techniques to persuade people with anorexia to indulge in a *small, pleasant food transgression* as a way to protect themselves from a loss of control: "If you indulge in it you can renounce it, but if you do not indulge in it, it will become compulsive". This evocative phrase has become an "invariant" form of therapeutic communication that together with a series of reasonings and reframings, allowed treatment-resistant patients to indulge in a small but pleasant transgression. This experience usually produced a "snowball effect" in which a tiny snowball, thrown in the right way, rolling without breaking on a suitable slope, gradually turns into an unstoppable mass.

In parallel with this, the importance of therapeutic work on the distorted aesthetic perception of people with anorexia was also tested. The goal was to create repulsion for an excessive weight loss by evoking "the beauty of being slim and the ugly of being skinny". This allowed patients to change the way they looked at themselves and to reduce the "deforming magnifying glass" effect that is typical of this disorder. In doing this, even people with the most serious anorexia began to eat and to perceive themselves more and more correctly, recovering both a sense of pleasure in food and a positive sense of self, as well as a sense of being desirable. Also, in this case, the efficacy of the therapy proved both very encouraging and superior to the results obtained by the other therapeutic approaches.

Since then, thousands of patients have come to Arezzo from every part of Italy to address their eating disorders, allowing us to continue to validate and expand these therapeutic techniques. Moreover, we have been able to refine the application of these therapeutic techniques to increase their effectiveness, to the point that this type of therapy provides highly satisfactory results in most cases. Efficacy now exceeds 80%, and the duration of treatments does not usually exceed 20 sessions, including follow-ups spanning more than two years after patients become asymptomatic, which typically occurs accomplished within ten sessions (i.e., within three–six months; Castelnuovo et al., 2010, 2019; Gibson, 2015; Gibson et al., 2016; Nardone & Watzlawick, 2005). Improvements can be seen in the first weeks of treatment, quickly reducing the health risks for patients.

Fifteen years from our initial research-intervention project and after an enormous amount of cases tackled by more than two hundred collaborators across the globe, we now find ourselves facing a further evolution of this pathology. In essence, we now see increasingly early onset, as well as early mutation (Istituto Superiore di Sanità – [National Institute of Health]) in the *vomiting* and *binge eating* variants, often associated with self-harming behaviours (Nardone & Selekman, 2011). We are seeing a kind of acceleration both of the onset and severity of the problem, which often escalates within a few months, with the loss of 10–15 kilograms over two to three months, along with other dangerous symptoms, particularly *vomiting*. Suffice it to say that average age of onset is now 11–12 years, in contrast to the previous average of 14–15 years. In addition, the Italian Society of Pediatrics highlights a worrisome tendency towards restricted eating behaviour starting as early as eight years old, especially in girls. Following this, the transition from the restrictive phase of the disorder to the compulsive phase takes place much more rapidly than has been observed in the past. That is to say that the stages are "skipped" and the voluntary execution of self-harming behaviour, such as cutting, burning, or scratching until the skin is harmed, is an increasingly frequent symptom of a restrictive eating disorder. This means that juvenile anorexia has become a more complex disorder in that, during the period of adolescence, the long-term evolutions of this eating pathology seen in adults are happening more quickly in adolescents. Even in the international scientific literature, this specific disorder is distinguished from adult anorexia, particularly due to the different therapeutic treatment required (Hay & McDermott, 2009; Le Grange et al., 2003; Lock, 2002; Nicholls & Bryant-Waugh, 2009; Robinson, 2001).

The modern evolution of family interaction models (Nardone et al., 2001), towards increasingly overprotective and permissive forms in the dynamics between parents and children, puts us in front of an increasing number of families made hostage by their daughter's eating disorder. In such situations, we see an almost total inability for families to manage the problem; this inability culminates in an ambivalent complicity that feeds the pathological phenomenon instead of reducing it.

Therefore, greater attention should be paid to early eating disorder cases. These should not be understood simply as precursors to the most serious cases that develop at a more advanced age; rather, they must be taken seriously as mental health disorders that require an *ad hoc* therapeutic intervention. In fact, the underestimation of these signs by families or healthcare professionals can very often allow the disorder to reach a chronic condition. In fact, we frequently observe 18-year-old adolescents with a long-term homeostatic eating pathology, structured as a real pathological homeostasis, highly resistant to therapeutic change that makes juvenile anorexia similar to the chronic anorexia of much older veterans of the disorder.

As already stated (but it is important to reiterate), the onset and evolution of this pathology have had a strong acceleration, opening the eyes of scholars and therapists to a far more serious reality than that encountered in previous decades. It is clear that tragic conditions can arise in a very short time, if we consider not only mortality but also the co-morbidities, the disorder reaching a chronic condition, and the lives of those imprisoned within anorexia.

Despite these hardly reassuring empirical observations, the therapeutic treatment, as we will try to illustrate in the following chapters, can also be rapid and able to bring about swift decreases in the dangerous symptomatology of anorexia. It can also be effective in building a psychological balance over time that helps prevent relapse. However, such an outcome is dependent on intervening on the interacting factors involved in the pathology – starting with the altered perceptions that produce the many distorted behavioural, emotional and cognitive reactions – and on family interactions complicit in the emergence and permanence of the disorder.

In 2013, to take stock of the knowledge and therapeutic modalities to cure modern juvenile anorexia, I held a seminar with Camillo Loriedo, one of the most eminent personalities in the field of eating disorders, in which we compared our methods. Loriedo is the director of a centre of excellence for the treatment of those eating disorders for which hospitalisation becomes inevitable due to physical risk. It was surprising for the participating colleagues, but also for the two of us, to notice that we agreed upon almost every aspect of the therapeutic treatment of juvenile anorexia. Although the contexts of hospitalisation and outpatient psychotherapy are quite different, the primary therapeutic goals and the strategies for obtaining them did not appear so dissimilar.

The reader should understand that usually the theme of eating disorders raises recurring, and often even fierce, theoretical and applicative disputes. However, when the goal is the fastest possible interruption of the disorder, the roads of those who actually work with the most severe cases tend to converge, highlighting some common and essential therapeutic factors for the successful outcome of treatments (Ball & Mitchell, 2004; Biondi & Loriedo, 2011; Le Grange et al., 2010; Lock et al., 2010; Nardone, 2003; Nardone & Selekman, 2011; Robin et al., 1994 1999; Russell et al., 1987; Vanderlinden, 2001). These factors, also confirmed by international scientific research (the Royal Australian and New Zealand College of Psychiatrists, 2014), have also emerged in a clear way from the research-intervention work that we have conducted in the last six years on this specific pathology at the Strategic Therapy Centre of Arezzo.

Therapeutic factors

- The parental role: parents have a fundamental part to play in therapeutic treatment, and sometimes they have to change their attitudes and behaviours in a radical way, ceasing to be "manipulators manipulated by their daughter", and instead assuming surprising and unforeseen positions in her eyes. The *Family Based Treatment*, as presented by Le Grange and his collaborators (2010) – resuming the seminal experience of the Maudsen Hospital, transforming parents from accomplices to co-therapists of the daughter's pathology — is a proven therapeutic technique for juvenile anorexia. For example, this entails making sure that parents remain at the table with their daughter until she has finished the agreed meal, without forcing her but also waiting for as long as it takes with calm and determination for her to finish her food. This methodology has demonstrated a high efficacy, to the point of becoming an *evidence-based* technique. At the level of communication, parents must overturn the double bind typical of the relationship with a daughter with anorexia: "If you love me let me, don't make me eat ... maybe until death"; by replying: "Even if I wanted to, I could not do that because I would be responsible for the damage to your health or for your death, so I apologise, but I will have to do what the doctors have said". In this way, it is the daughter who becomes "the manipulated manipulator hostage of the parents", who are obligated by their role to prevent her from continuing her deadly trajectory because doing so would make them consciously guilty.

- Evocation of sensations: making the patient "feel" rather than "understand" plays a crucial role. This is about working on creating different sensations towards food and towards one's own body instead of offering rational explanations about the disorder. Persuading them to change as an alternative to convincing them to heal, through suggestive and sometimes hypnotic communication techniques, which are able both to create feelings of aversion to those behaviours that nourish the pathology, and to instead amplify those that promote therapeutic change. In this way, the patient's perceptions and reactions are transformed, from pathological to healthy, by circumventing resistance to change instead of opposing it.

This means overcoming purely instructive and directive techniques aimed at modifying cognitions and eating behaviours, in favour of suggestive-persuasive techniques aimed at transforming perceptions and emotions towards food and one's own body, to induce change in eating behaviour.

A very important feature of the advanced treatment of juvenile anorexia is the focus on *evoking the pleasure of the dreaded foods*, by using powerfully evocative and shared images during the therapeutic dialogue, to mobilise the most primitive sensations, which represent a major key to unlocking the sealed strongbox of anorexic pathology. The therapist must talk about the foods that the girl would love to eat, "as if" they would not make her gain weight, by using proper hypnotic suggestions to reactivate the senses deadened from repeated abstinence and excessive slimming. It is known, in fact, that, under a certain weight threshold, cortical activities are strongly compromised, so that those suffering from severe cases of anorexia are not able to sustain a reasoned dialogue, although they still respond to the stimuli of the most primitive sensations, such as pleasure and fear. Therefore, hypnotic techniques represent, in effect, a proven and powerful therapeutic tool for eating disorders (Vanderlinden, 2001).

It is clear that, from this point of view, the equation *food = medicine*, which is the predominant communicative modality of psychiatric cognitive-behavioural approaches in the treatment of anorexia, not only fails, but it can be counter-productive. In fact, this methodology, associated with the concept of mechanical feeding, to which patients must become accustomed, even when completed, cannot be considered healing, but rather a "sad management of the pathology". In fact, patients who can comply with this type of eating behaviour rarely come out of their rigid obsessive cognitive schema of food control and continue to perceive food as a dangerous demon to be kept closed inside the cage of medicalisation; therefore, in most cases, they remain hostage to the disorder. Moreover, as well documented by research, the majority end up slipping into *binge eating* or *vomiting*, precisely because of the rigid diet to which they are subjected: excessive control leads mostly to a loss of control, as happens in all obsessive-compulsive disorders (Nardone & Valteroni, 2014; Nardone et al., 2005). This also applies to therapeutic programmes that are rigidly regulated, for example through inflexible nutritional patterns, and which run the risk of leading to a total loss of control, promoting the consequent onset of advanced forms of the disorder, based on the fight against inevitable *binge eating*.

The only true healing from an eating pathology is reached when a person attains a healthy body weight and is satisfied with their shape, eating what they like and finding that this is not only not risky, but that it keeps them in balance, at a place where they can like themselves and feel that they are liked by others (Nardone, 2007). Anything else is only management of the pathology in patients at risk of a new symptomatic exacerbation.

- Hospitalisation: hospitalisation to enable force-feeding should only be the last resort to save a life or to avoid serious physiological damage to patients who are dangerously underweight, and should not be standard procedure, as often happens. When hospitalisation is deemed necessary, it should be short (i.e., never more than a few weeks) to avoid triggering a tug-of-war between forced therapy and the strenuous resistance of patients. In fact, it is often the case that patients with anorexia, once released from a prolonged hospital stay, start again with the usual pathological modalities, if not with evolutions of the disorder learned during the hospitalisation. In many cases, young patients learn to vomit, perform self-harming acts or use anorectic medications from other inpatients during hospitalisation.

One should bear in mind that by gathering young anorexic patients together, as it is usually done in self-help groups or in specialised clinics, one runs the risk of creating the "group-belonging effect", which is well known in social psychology but not so much considered by institutional psychiatry. The creation of strong group cohesion around anorexia strengthens its attractive value by virtue of feeling loyal to the group. This can, therefore, create a sort of devotees' sect to the "goddess" anorexia. Such an evolution is more likely the younger the patients and the less developed their sense of identity as they are at elevated risk for defining their identity around a shared eating pathology. This becomes a tempting dysfunctional solution to manage self-esteem problems and emotional and relational comparison problems that are typical of adolescents but are even more relevant to those adolescents suffering from similar disorders.

However, one should not overlook the fact that cohesion and adherence to the reference group can also become an important therapeutic resource when one is able to strongly orientate the group towards shared therapeutic results, as a group of people works better than the single person to achieve difficult goals (Loriedo, 2013). For this reason, it is important for those who manage the group to have a great ability to influence it in the direction of healing rather than in the maintenance of the disorder. In such cases, the psychotherapist's charisma and powers of persuasion are fundamental.

Based on observations resulting from a careful and rigorous clinical trial, we have formalised a protocol of specific treatment for juvenile anorexia aimed at breaking the rigidity of the pathological situation from the very first session with the patient and their family, thanks to the application of specific therapeutic stratagems and a suggestive and evocative *ad hoc* communication. Once the resistant mechanism of the disorder is weakened, the young patient is led to build a stable balance over time, based on gratification for food, her own appearance, and confidence in her own resources.

As we will see in more detail, if the treatment works one will immediately observe an unlocking of the eating restriction or of the other variants of the disorder, such as *vomiting* or *binge eating*. This will be followed by a slow and progressive acquisition of new, functional modes of self-perception concerning the relationship with one's own body and with others and the management of emotions, in parallel with the restoring of body weight. This is accompanied by a modification of dysfunctional family dynamics.

In these cases, follow-ups are prolonged for about two years after the actual elimination of the disorder in patients and represent a necessary part of the therapy to consolidate the results obtained and to ensure they are persistent in their recovery. We like to define this treatment as a long-term brief therapy.

Notes

1 Although it is possible to trace the clinical descriptions of eating disorders back many years, these made their first entry into DSM classification in 1980, as a subcategory of disorders of childhood or early adolescence. It was not until DSM-4 that they were classified as a separate category (1994).
2 This idea was strongly supported by psycho-dynamic psychotherapy approaches and still imposes on the most orthodox therapists to not manage problematic behaviours directly, as they are considered an expression of unconscious conflicts and functional to the maintenance of one's psychological equilibrium.

Chapter 3

Understanding the disorder

Before proceeding with the presentation of the therapy model that we have formulated, it seems necessary to present an overview of the disorder, highlighting the more frequently associated characteristics, variants, and symptoms.

Pure juvenile anorexia

Pure juvenile anorexia presents with a marked restriction in both the quantity and quality of food consumed, often disguised, in the initial stages, by a healthy or vegetarian ideological choice. The condition is that of significant, and typically rapid, weight loss.[1] In this variant of the disorder, we do not observe a compulsion towards physical exercise, because a muscular form is also rejected: the ideal is a threadlike body. The obsession is that of skinniness in association with a phobia of being fat or heavy. Over time, self-worth is increasingly determined based on what weight scales and appearance say. Some girls see themselves as "fat" all over; others, while admitting their overall state of thinness, find some body parts, often the abdomen, hips, buttocks, and thighs, hideously large. In most cases, they view their own bodies with deep shame and a concern for what others may think of their appearance. Many adolescent girls do not let other people observe or touch them; they are the first to avoid looking at themselves. Conversely, others will constantly inspect their physical shape in front of the mirror. Almost none will wear swimsuits, tight-fitting clothes or clothes that leave the body parts considered "too large" uncovered; almost all will avoid going to the beach or swimming pools. Girls with the pure variant of juvenile anorexia are very self-critical and tend to systematically overestimate others and underestimate themselves. They feel inadequate on a personal and social level, especially in their relationships with their peers. At the level of interpersonal relationships, a gradual social withdrawal can be observed, allowing the girls to avoid the "risk" of social situations where a loss of control over dietary restriction could occur. This behaviour tends to become radical, culminating in the refusal to eat in the presence of other people, including family members.

The paradoxical phenomenon that disrupts families and is so shocking to the layperson is a progressive body dysmorphia[2] generated in parallel with weight loss. That is to say, "the slimmer they become, the fatter or heavier they believe themselves to be", as if they wore magnifying lenses. This distorted self-perception triggers an even more pronounced reduction in food intake, and is in turn boosted by it, in a pathological vicious cycle that can lead to the most unfortunate outcomes. This perceptual and behavioural dynamic is associated with another subtle and even more powerful one: that every form of pleasure is experienced as a potentially dangerous loss of control. At first, this happens only with food, but after a short time young anorexic girls tend to avoid everything that can disturb their "heavenly" balance, so as to inhibit even the natural sexual drives typical of early adolescence. On the contrary, these girls are extremely attentive to obligations and commitments in areas in which they are very competitive. They strive to be the best in the class and the most diligent, so much so that they often take their academic dedication to excess by eliminating any other activity, including reducing sleep, until they reach physical and mental exhaustion. A characteristic sign of the advanced phases of weight loss is, in fact, a reduced ability to concentrate, to the point where mere reading or listening may cause extreme fatigue. In the most severe cases, giving up their studies that they care so much about becomes almost inevitable. Cognitive abilities stiffen with the worsening of the pathology and thinking becomes dichotomous (black and white). Perfectionism in areas of interest leads those affected to experience all that falls just short of perfection as a sort of failure; at the same time, this "failure" strengthens their poor self-perception and leads them to avoid situations that cannot be perfectly managed. All this causes the pathology to manifest as a rigid and unalterable way of perceiving reality, to which patients react with equally uncompromising thoughts and actions. Anorexia is an armour worn to defend oneself that turns into a prison from which the young girl with pure juvenile anorexia cannot free herself: spontaneous remissions are very rare and, on closer examination, show that something happened in the life of these girls which has therapeutically upset their rigid pathological balance. Given such a complex clinical situation, it would seem obvious for the therapy to be equally complicated: this is, in fact, the linear logical deduction which for decades has led to the practice of forms of treatment sometimes even more complex than the pathology itself, and with unsatisfactory results. Non-linear formal logic, as well as clinical experience, shows instead how the best therapeutic solution for a complex clinical problem is an apparently simple intervention, but one which is aimed at immediately breaking the inflexible psychological and relational patterns that feed the pathology.

Juvenile anorexia with *exercising*

This variant of juvenile anorexia can be distinguished by the fact that, from the point of view of pathological behaviour, it is characterised by a compulsion to exercise in order to burn calories, in addition to a reduced food intake. This attempted solution to avoid weight-gain from eating, or as a way of ensuring continued weight loss with the same eating regimen, can become so pervasive as to actually override the symptomatology of the food intake restriction. Sometimes, this type of patient with anorexia will accept an increase of food without excessive resistance, but not a reduction of motor activity. In many cases, they are never still and take advantage of every opportunity to move and burn calories: going up and down the stairs, walking for hours relentlessly, and repeating strenuous exercises hundreds of times – especially those to reduce the perceived size of the belly. The main physical activity is aerobic and may be disguised as sports practice that requires hard training, such as endurance sports or dance. The picture is that of a debilitating compulsive obsession that, when it reaches its extremes, does not allow the person to do anything but constantly fight against the fear of gaining weight by burning calories through movement. Injuries such as tendonitis, gonalgia, heel pain, and muscular damage are frequent; these, however, do not halt the excessive exercise. In this regard, we recall a prime example for which a colleague, who worked in a Californian hospital specialising in the treatment of anorexia, requested consultation. A girl had been admitted to the hospital because she had reached the dangerous weight of 33 kilograms and, despite having agreed to eat over 2000 Kcal per day, she was still not gaining weight. The colleague was asked whether the girl was carrying out a motor activity or adopting other compensation methods, such as taking laxatives or *vomiting*. He reported that she was supervised throughout the day and that nothing of the sort had been noticed. He was then asked whether the hospital staff could verify what she was doing at night. The mystery was thus revealed: every night she was walking up and down the hospital fire escape. As illustrated in this example, these patients show a dogged determination to carry out the activities that they consider to be essential in order to maintain a physical shape which they consider reassuring. The majority of clinicians and eating disorder treatment models consider hyperactivity a significant but non-specific symptom, and only an expression of the desire to lose weight or to avoid gaining weight. However, in accordance with some authors (Dalle Grave, 2015), we believe that this is a specific and decisive factor in the maintenance and aggravation of the eating problem; therefore, it requires a different therapy from that adopted with pure juvenile anorexia. Also, to corroborate the clinical evidence, the results of some controlled studies in the animal world have shown that an excess of physical activity can lead one to stop eating even when food is abundant. That is, a vicious cycle takes shape in which the more the levels of movement increase, the more the drive to eat decreases. These biological mechanisms result in a further increase in the levels of movement. It is, then, clear that in anorexia with *exercising*, the simple reinstatement of an adequate eating regimen does not represent healing but only an improvement of the pathological condition, which is achievable with the therapeutic process described in the next chapter.

Juvenile anorexia with *binge eating*

More than two-thirds of people with anorexia cannot maintain long-term food restriction and yield to the temptation to eat, often becoming overwhelmed by desire for the foods which they have forbidden. When this occurs, it is devastating for those who have made their ability to abstain from food – especially from the "tastiest" of foods – the backbone of their struggle to control their "all too human impulses". However, in the days following the descent into loss of control, an even greater restriction of nutrient intake seems like a good solution to these girls and, in fact, most of the time this is practised. But as the "abstinent saints" soon discover, this "reasonable" strategy to retake control over the tempting food-demon leads to a new trap: the alternation of food restriction and *binge eating* in a perverse vicious circle, in which *binge eating* forces greater restriction, which in turn leads to a new loss of control. One behaviour supports another in perfect pathological complementarity. Thus, anorexia is plagued by *binge eating* and this gives rise to a variant of the disorder characterised by periods of hyper-control followed by colossal binges that can last entire days. Some patients may eat so much that they must then rest for hours like a snake that has swallowed a large prey, waiting to digest the food. However, in juvenile anorexia with *binge eating*, the situation mostly does not completely transform into the clear picture of a pathology characterised by uncontrolled eating; usually, it remains in a phase where abstinence alternates with loss of control, and this is usually not extreme. However, for a girl with restrictive anorexia, even eating something that they have deemed "not allowed" represents a binge that, to their mind, must be compensated. This means that restricted food intake remains the dominant symptomatology, although this is no longer well-managed. Certainly, if the disorder is not treated and overcome, it will typically evolve into the *binge eating* or *vomiting* variations. However, it should be stressed that, when it is possible to intervene within an appropriate timeframe, the fact that the girl has lost control over her restricted food intake is used as an important lever for the benefit of the therapeutic treatment.

Juvenile anorexia with *vomiting*

As already stated in other texts (Nardone, 2003; Nardone & Selekman, 2011; Nardone et al., 2005), this variant represents the most frequent evolution of the pathology and it is likely to become an even more complex, disabling, and risky disorder in patients' lives. In fact, self-induced *vomiting* leads to electrolyte imbalance, which is the most frequent cause of death in eating disorders. Initially, the pathological behaviour comes from wanting to "reasonably" compensate for having eaten more than what is perceived as acceptable. For instance, for a teenager with restrictive anorexia, eating more than "necessary" can consist of eating one spoonful too many or by feeling swollen. Then, precisely because these girls perceive *vomiting* as an effective remedy for having eaten too much, they usually allow themselves to break their strict diet, increasingly enjoying eating. In this way, they become victims of the compulsion to eat and vomit and they increase the quantity of food eaten and the frequency of binges followed by *vomiting*. In the most serious cases, they come to spend entire days binging and *vomiting* (Nardone & Selekman, 2011; Nardone et al., 2005). In other words, because *vomiting* is extremely satisfying it tends to evolve, from a "good solution" to avoid gaining weight or even lose weight while eating more than deemed permissible to an irrepressible pleasurable compulsion. The desire to binge eat may go so far as to monopolise the thoughts of these young patients, and their deliberate planning of the perfect moment in which to carry it out can lead them to give up seeing peers, miss taking part in extracurricular activities, or to skip school without their parents' permission. Usually, families try to contain the frequency and intensity of the episodes by hiding food, but they soon realise that no hiding place is safe, and that all sorts of food, even frozen food or dry bread, may be considered edible. Patients reach a point where they plan what they will eat and subsequently regurgitate, and when they do not have money they may steal food from shops; this happens even when they are normally socially compliant and very attentive to other people's needs. This has nothing to do with self-destructive behaviours highlighted by various authors (Levitt et al., 2004; Waller, 1992; Zerbe, 2008); instead, this is a deliberate search for transgressive pleasure that has a destructive effect rather than a destructive intent. It is this intrinsic characteristic that makes it the most resistant among eating disorders. In clinical practice, two distinct stages of the disorder are observed:

- First, the young girl with anorexia vomits because she thinks she has eaten too much, and in this case, *vomiting* is the remedy. Second, the young adolescent stuffs herself in order to vomit, and in this case, *vomiting* is the final part of a pleasure-based pattern.

This may astonish the reader, but to paraphrase Francis Bacon: "Thin is the line between disgust and pleasure". Usually, the first variant evolves into the second one over a few months if the episodes of *vomiting* escalate and become a daily routine. If it is possible to intervene in the first developmental stage of the disorder when the anorexic mindset is still prevalent, then eliminating the compulsion to vomit will be easier both for the patient and

18 Understanding the disorder

for the therapist. However, if the patient is already totally at the second developmental stage, the therapy becomes more complex: (1) because of the type of relationship and communication that needs to be established with these cases are difficult to manage (patients are often provocative, seductive, rejecting, and uncooperative); and (2) because of the therapeutic expediency that needs to be adopted to break the vicious circle of such a strongly structured pathology. We have been dealing with this type of disorder for more than 20 years and we have formalised a specific treatment with therapeutic variants adapted to the different characteristics of both the pathology and the patients.

Juvenile anorexia with *self-harming*

Another variation of the disorder, often associated with *vomiting* (Nardone & Selekman, 2011), is characterised by *self-harming* behaviour, such as cutting oneself with knives, razors, and other sharp objects, piercing with needles and blades, burning oneself with cigarette butts or candles, or by rubbing, scratching with one's own fingernails, hitting oneself, pinching oneself to the point of drawing blood and, finally, tearing one's own hair and skin. None of these forms tend to self-destructiveness or result from suicidal intentions (Favaro et al., 2004); instead, they either function like a sedative in relation to negative emotional states, such as increased tension, boredom, anxiety, pain, or they represent the pursuit of a subtle pleasure. In fact, such acts are performed in times of crisis to discharge tension, as the sensation of pain dulls the ongoing emotion; few practices are so effective in eliminating emotional suffering. Alternatively, such practices may represent a deliberate pursuit of the thrill produced by the painful act which, if repeated, turns into a form of pleasure. This effect may seem unnatural, but it is our physiology, at least in part, to ensure that a small torture replicated over time evolves into something pleasant. Masochistic behaviours, in fact, have been known since ancient times. It is essential to know that, at an epidemiological level, *self-harming* behaviour without suicidal intention is associated with anorexic eating disorder in more than 70% of cases. It is thus considered a common symptom in the more severe forms of this pathology (Selekman, 2005, 2009). Through research-intervention in this clinical area, we have developed a specific therapeutic strategy over the years that, in most cases, must accompany those used for the treatment of pure juvenile anorexia or one of its variants, especially *vomiting* and the multi-symptomatic variant.

Juvenile anorexia with *elimination*

Among the pathological behaviours related to anorexia, those characterised by the use of laxatives, enemas, and other practices to facilitate intestinal evacuation, as well as the use of diuretics, are among the most well-known and noted. The frequency of laxative use is currently declining compared to past decades, perhaps as a result of the side effects becoming more widely known. Instead, the use of water-based enemas or enemas based on substances such as chamomile is increasingly widespread. Such usage stems from the belief that this practice helps to purify the intestine and will not cause iatrogenic damage. The abuse of diuretics is also increasingly frequent; conversely, the age at which they start to be used is decreasing. This escalation may be associated with "exotic" eating habits or new diets influenced by the eastern world. As we have already mentioned, these behaviours often represent the waiting room, if not the doorway, to the restrictive eating disorder or its orthorexic variant (i.e., the fixation on those foods considered "healthy" and the phobic avoidance of those that are "non-healthy"). Most of the time, this picture evolves into mental anorexia. Although the majority of laxatives work at the level of the small intestine and not of the large intestine, where the absorption of food takes place, the belief that their use allows people to avoid gaining weight unfortunately is still widespread. From a clinical point of view, the real problem is the fact that the repeated laxative use tends to structure a more psychological and physiological dependence; therefore, the young anorexic sufferer feels reassured by their use, even in the face of evidence of only minimal weight loss. The use of enemas, if repeated over time, has another subtle but influential effect: the stimulation of sensitive mucous membranes tends to structure pleasant transgressive compulsions, which are difficult to extinguish. Diuretic preparations, always abused to excess by anorexic users, often with the declared intent to expel toxins, also have a duplicitous result: as they facilitate diuresis, they give anorexia sufferers the impression of losing weight, which is why young patients are not willing to easily suspend their use. These two joint effects determine the success of these practices associated with restrictive eating behaviour and at the same time demonstrate their effective dangerousness. It should be stressed that the consequences of these behaviours are too often underestimated not only by family members but also by specialists, who sometimes even suggest the use of similar remedies or do not try hard enough to suspend their use. However, in our clinical and research experience, we have observed that this is of great importance, since such dysfunctional behaviours are not secondary to the eating disorder but rather are powerful autonomous elements of maintenance and aggravation of the pathology itself.

Juvenile anorexia with *substance abuse*

In this case, we are not facing a variant but a form of dangerous pathological behaviour that frequently adds to the restrictive eating disorder, the *vomiting* disorder, and the multi-symptomatic disorder. The use of chemicals such as ipecac[3] syrup to induce *vomiting*, drugs such as amphetamines and derivatives, and medicines or galenic products that through inhibitory processes allow one to not feel hunger is a worrying phenomenon. The reasons why this phenomenon is worrying are the enormous spread of drugs in increasingly young age groups and the ease of using the internet to obtain products forbidden to minors on traditional markets. In the last two decades, there has been a sharp increase in the use of chemical aids by those who believe that dieting, *vomiting*, and *exercising* will not be enough to maintain their desired physical shape. Where illegal drugs are concerned, the most valued are hyper-stimulants such as amphetamine and all its derivatives because they allow one to be active without experiencing fatigue or hunger. Such as anorectic drugs, these are surprisingly frequently prescribed to patients who report difficulties in following a diet and to those who are slightly overweight. This is done without assessing the dangerous effects in terms of lack of control over food consumption and the subsequent possible development of anorexia, of which these drugs become an essential component. Another worrying element is that these substances are often available through a sort of black market in gyms and weight loss centres, where they may be sold in the form of galenic preparations at exorbitant prices. Certainly, those who deal in them become veritable dealers, making money by inducing an authentic chemical and psychological dependence, into which girls desperate to lose weight could easily fall. Finally, some psychotropic drugs, such as topiramate, seem to cause weight reduction, which is why a non-trivial number of young anorexic sufferers try to have it prescribed. If users do not comply with the therapeutic dosage, these drugs can have dangerous health consequences. However, pharmacology applied to eating disorders[4] is rarely effective, particularly concerning children and adolescents under 18. No compound has yet been approved for the pharmacotherapy of anorexia, whereas only fluoxetine alone has been approved by the Food and Drug Administration for the treatment of bulimia (Dalle Grave, 2015; Faravelli, 2010; NCCMH, 2004; Steffen et al., 2007). In conclusion, when substance use and abuse is detected in a patient, it is necessary to intervene with a process of physiological detoxification while working in parallel to release the patient from their psychological dependence to optimise the results of the treatment of the eating disorder.

Polysymptomatic juvenile anorexia and/or borderline personality disorder

In the daily clinical practice of eating disorders, another condition can be observed in addition to the forms of juvenile anorexia already described in which more than one variant of the disorder is co-occurring. In other words, patients are frequently found exhibiting all the different pathological behaviours related to food, which alternate over time. It almost seems like a kind of experimentation, searching for the best method to avoid gaining or losing weight. The polysymptomatic variant of juvenile anorexia can be found in cases where the disorder has a long history, despite the young age of the patients. This is because when early intervention is possible, the eating disorder usually has less varied or oligosymptomatic forms. However, even chronic sufferers of anorexia, although still adolescents, after having experienced different dysfunctional modes of managing food and bodyweight, tend to crystallise on the mode that is most functional to their pathological equilibrium. This means that one of the pathological variants associated with food restriction becomes dominant: those sufferers whose variants evolved through *vomiting* have binges and *vomiting* as prevalent practices; those with variants that turn into *binge eating* alternate binges and restricted food intake as their main mode; and those with variants associated with *exercising* focus on excessive motor activity. This is an important clinical evaluation, as it orientates the precise therapeutic intervention which will be needed to stop the dominant expression of the disorder. This, in fact, represents the architecture of persistence and aggravation of the disease. Accurate assessment is essential to make rapid and radical therapeutic changes in pathologies based on rigid forms of control or on uncontrollable compulsions. This is because, by means of strategies aimed at disrupting the twisted game of the predominant symptomatology, a proper snowball effect can be produced which crushes the entire pathological mechanism. To conclude our description of the different variants of the eating disorder in puberty and adolescence, we must mention a common connection made in the specialist literature between borderline personality disorder and eating pathology, in particular with regard to *vomiting*, anorexia with self-harm, and anorexia with substance use. In the most severe forms, a multi-symptomatic picture may be found in which frequent binges followed by *vomiting* are accompanied by *self-harming* behaviour. The latter can escalate to suicide threats, use and abuse of drugs or alcohol, kleptomania, sexual promiscuity, and other impulsive behaviour, to the point of suggesting a general deficit in the control of impulses (Costa et al., 2011; Lacey & Evans, 1986; Safer et al., 2009; Wonderlich et al., 2002) and the presence of a borderline personality disorder. However, this is a nosographic picture that presents some critical points. Firstly, the construct of personality disorder is not universally recognised. Secondly, a unique definition of the criteria required for a borderline diagnosis is lacking. Moreover, according to the international classifications of DSM-5 and ICD, it would not be possible to diagnose a personality disorder until the onset of adulthood or at least until the age of 18. In contrast, in clinical practice and in books, a certain percentage of cases with eating pathology are frequently associated with a borderline personality disorder. The clinical evidence is provided by typical multi-symptomatic patients who, in addition to dysfunctional eating behaviours, present high and pervasive instability of emotions, of their self-image and interpersonal relationships – oscillating between the extremes of idealisation and the devaluation of themselves and others – difficulties in controlling anger and impulses, and chronic feelings of emptiness and boredom. These young women have great difficulty in setting goals and maintaining them, and this, together with marked mood reactivity, strongly interferes with the construction of an integrated sense of self. Many authors hypothesise that borderline personality disorder is the pathological background to which eating disorders are grafted, thus determining a greater level of severity in terms of symptoms and prognosis. We believe that, in the majority of cases, it is the eating disorder that, when prolonged or chronic, can give rise to a borderline picture. This is because the disorder develops at an age where one of the fundamental tasks of development is precisely the structuring of a stable sense of identity, distinct from that of childhood. However, several authors emphasise how food restriction and dysfunctional conduct related to food can alter the functioning of personality (Dalle Grave, 2015; Keys et al., 1950; Lilenfeld, 2004; Nardone et al., 2005). This is evidenced by the fact that these patients, once healed from their eating disorder, no longer have the necessary characteristics to formulate a diagnosis of borderline disorder (Dalle Grave, 2015; Nardone & Selekman, 2011).

Notes

1 The diagnostic standard of body weight is at the centre of a heated debate. In fact, in addition to undergoing weight loss, young anorexic patients who are still physically developing may also be unable to reach their expected adult weight or to maintain a trajectory of normal development. For this reason, BMI (Body Mass Index, calculated as weight in kilograms/height in metres squared) percentiles are increasingly used, as they allow BMI values to be interpreted according to age group.
2 The literature on body image distortion is very broad and includes several explanatory hypotheses. For a long time, in fact, scholars have wondered what such a bizarre dysmorphia could indicate – if it is the outcome of malnutrition and metabolic alteration and whether it is necessary to modify it in order to achieve healing. In recent years, neuropsychological and neuroscience research has contributed to our understanding, but an exhaustive explanation of the phenomenon has yet to be reached.
3 Chronic ipecac consumption results in a myopathy that affects striated muscles, including the heart. Ipecac contains, in fact, emetine, a cardiotoxic substance that can provoke sudden death. In addition, ipecac syrup is hepatotoxic and causes weakness in peripheral muscles.
4 Most of the research results in the field of pharmacological treatment for eating disorders stems from studies carried out on samples of adult patients, therefore they have important limitations. In fact, pharmacokinetic differences between adults and children/adolescents are known, which means that processes of absorption, metabolism, distribution, and elimination of substances change considerably according to age.

Chapter 4

Therapeutic treatment

Breaking the patterns of juvenile anorexia

When dealing with a dangerous psychological and behavioural pathology such as anorexia, being able to intervene quickly to stop its disastrous development is crucial. It must be considered that, in addition to the aforementioned mortality rate, being severely underweight and self-provoking physiological stresses produce sometimes irreversible damage to major internal organs. Therefore, the first objective must be to stop the vicious circle that is maintaining the problem.

Although it may seem obvious, this is an important element to emphasise. In fact, therapies related to anorexia often support, in a dogmatic way, the idea that to overcome a pathology so deeply rooted as anorexia, it is necessary to unearth its "deep causes", instead of immediately tackling its dangerous symptomatology. This is very risky when dealing with girls who are severely underweight and whose actions, such as excessive *exercising*, binge-eating, purging, and *self-harming* behaviours have significant damaging effects. On a theoretical-applicative level, a clinical distinction between original causes and symptoms is flawed. Although this distinction finds explanation in psychodynamic approaches, it is ill-suited to pathologies in which the symptomatology corresponds to the disorder and the disorder has clear causes and evolutions without needing to uncover the causes underlying the disorder.

Having clarified this, we can move on to illustrate the first phase of an effective and efficient treatment for juvenile anorexia. The first session with the patient and her family represents a decisive phase for the outcome of the therapy. In fact, in most cases, the way we manage the first session will define whether or not we will succeed in therapeutic intervention. In part, this is because, in most cases, the young candidate patients are reluctant to be "cured" since they believe they are pursuing a worthy goal. Therefore, in the first session we must be able to persuade them that their condition is in fact pathological and in need of a cure. Moreover, we need to apply techniques that can trigger a change in the situation as regards both family dynamics complicit in the problem, and the perceptions and behaviour of the girl toward food and toward her own body.

Structure of the first session

The opening lines of the therapeutic session must address the *investigation of the disorder*. This is carried out firstly through a series of perceptive questions, which accurately identify the type of anorexic eating disorder, and confirm the fact-finding and diagnostic observations through paraphrasing. The paraphrasing technique is based on providing a summary and evaluation of the answers given by the patient, thereby seeking agreement between patient and therapist. Thus, it is a method for creating an effective therapeutic relationship.

Once the type of problem has been identified, the next therapeutic manoeuvre is *a reframing of the responsibility of the parents* with respect to the health of their daughter and the potential deterioration of her condition, including the most unfortunate possible outcome. In such cases, the girl may hold her parents "hostage" through emotional blackmail, ensuring that they coalesce to her demands. Through the therapeutic manoeuvre, parents are made guardians of the well-being of their underage daughter with regard to her anorexia; they are held accountable to concrete responsibilities. In this way, they regain their parental authority over their daughter and can avoid the guilt of being complicit in her dangerous pathology. After having redefined the family dynamics, we agree with the parents that, if their daughter's weight loss reaches a particular threshold of risk, which can vary from person to person, they must take her immediately to a hospital for forced feeding. In doing this, we also talk directly to the patient and explain what would happen in this scenario, using a *strongly evocative image*: "They will insert a tube through your nose and blow you up like a balloon". This suggestive technique is repeated several times to obtain an overload-effect. It is a bit like predicting what the young anorexic patient would like to avoid – that is, to be forced to regain weight quickly.

A new climate has emerged, both for the parents and for the daughter, who now becomes, in turn, a hostage to her own actions and to the inevitable reaction of her parents, who are now bound to their medical responsibilities. At this point we proceed by proposing a sort of *illusion of alternative*:

> You can avoid all this if you agree to gradually regain half a kilogram per week, no more than this ... Otherwise there will be a tube that will blow you up like a balloon and you will regain several kilograms all at once. Of course, you might be thinking that after that you could start losing weight again, but then there will be the tube again and it will blow you up like a balloon ... If you agree to gradually and slowly regain half a kilogram per week, we can plan together how to achieve this and help you reach your target weight without making you gain a single gram more.

Technically, this is called a "therapeutic double bind" and it is a powerful technique to make the unacceptable acceptable. Once this crucial step is achieved, the attitude of the girl is usually resigned and accepting. At this point, we completely change our communicative and relational register. We propose directly to her a *suggestive dialogue* about what she would really like to eat, *as if the desired food would not make her gain weight*. She is asked to draw up a *top ten* list, using *strongly evocative images about the pleasure of tasting* for each food. This technique represents a strategy to awaken and draw out the sense of pleasure from eating that she has denied herself.

After conquering the bastion of resistance of the young anorexic patient we start to negotiate in detail *all that she will have to eat, meal by meal, over the following week*. Transforming what has been established during the clinical session into an action plan is essential for the therapeutic effects to be concretely realised.

Finally, a further, unavoidable form of agreement concerns the fact that *parents will need to stay at the table with their daughter, without talking about food and without forcing her in any way*, until the end of each meal; moreover, at least one parent must stay with her for at least another hour afterwards to prevent clandestine *vomiting* or immediate *exercising*. The following is a literal transcript of a first therapeutic session.

First session explanatory example

Before me, a silent anorexic girl sits stiffly between her parents. For over two months she has refused to eat anything but fruit, and that only in increasingly smaller quantities. In the previous six months she has gradually reduced her diet and has lost over 20 kilograms. She now weighs only 33 kilograms, with a height of 169 cm: she is in serious danger of death. The girl has already been subjected to two forced feeding hospitalisations that have made her gain a few kilograms, but these were systematically "burned off" a few days after her release from hospital.

After hearing the case history and the attempts put in place to resolve it, I ask the parents if it is clear enough that, as their daughter is a minor, they must be considered responsible for her health and that, therefore, they will be responsible for every bad thing that could happen to her. The strategy has the desired effect, and the girl intervenes by saying that her parents are not at fault, because it is she who does not want to eat. I reply: "Sure, but with the best intentions they have produced the worst results: by standing with you, by complying with your wishes, they have allowed you to come to this point." She insists: "No, it's all my fault!" "Your fault, or your disorder's?" I counter. Surprised, she responds: "My disease's". I ask: "Let me get this straight, if it is your illness and not you who wants this, should we allow it or fight it?" "I should fight it, but it's stronger than me," the girl answers. "Maybe I could help you fight it if you let me," I say. And she: "I would, but I don't know if I will be able to do it, because I'm so afraid of getting fat …" "Ok. Nobody mentioned that. Of course, if we want to save

26   Therapeutic treatment

you we have to get your weight up, but that does not mean getting fat" I reply, and she nods.

As we can see, such a rapid and intense verbal and non-verbal exchange created a collaborative contact where before there was resolute resistance. The girl began to contemplate the idea of resuming a "healthy weight", something that was previously inconceivable for her, as doing it was equal to "getting fat". It was possible to reach this point by using orientating questions to separate the patient from her illness.

"Good, if I am not mistaken, we have a common enemy to fight: your illness that makes you afraid to eat in case you get fat." She nods again, and I proceed: "I must warn you, it will not be painless or easy but, if you help me to help you, we will make it". Tears appear in her eyes as she nods.

"Good. Now I have to ask you a really critical question," I tell her, looking intensely into her eyes.

> Would you prefer to start eating again very gradually, by choosing together which foods you can allow yourself, and regain no more than half a kilogram per week, or, as your parents will be forced to do due to their direct responsibility for you, would you prefer to be subjected again to forced feeding, but this time in an intensive way so that you gain several kilograms very quickly?

I press the matter: "In other words, would you prefer to put on weight by eating gradually and pleasantly, or to have a tube up your nose that blows you up like a balloon?"

The girl, as usually happens in such situations, chooses the first option to avoid the second one, which is to her mind far worse. What was previously impossible was made possible by a process of therapeutic persuasion: as a result of a single strategic dialogue a patient with very serious anorexia, agrees to resume eating and gain weight.

After this first fundamental agreement, we proceed to define in detail what the girl will eat.

> As we have agreed to fight our enemy, we must now agree on how to deal with food. At this point, let me ask you another question: if you could eat without fear, what would you like to eat more than anything? Let's make a ranked list of the tastiest foods for you …

There is an evident dilation of pupils, the sign of her pleasure mechanisms activating, and she says: "Pizza!" I reply: "Soft crust or thin?" She: "Thin and very crunchy that so that it crackles between your teeth." And I carry on: "With hot, stringy mozzarella cheese or with a lot of overflowing tomato sauce?" "With hot, stringy mozzarella cheese!"

The evocation of images of her favourite food triggers genuine pleasure in the patient. Research shows (Doidge, 2016) that guided imagery produces sensory effects that are not unlike the real ones. This is a powerful vehicle for change, especially when it is adopted with people who no longer allow themselves pleasure because of fear.

Together, we draw up a ranked list of her favourite foods, and together we decide what to start with when she resumes eating, so as to avoid regaining more than half a kilogram each week.

The parents are briefed thus: "You have the important task of arranging the agreed foods, making them available on the table and staying with her until the end of the meal, without talking about her problem and without insisting that she eats". I then repeat that they will have to stay there until she has finished and for some time after. "Then, at least one of you will have to stay with her for the next two hours to talk or to do some activities, such as clearing the table …"

Second phase: from the second to the fifth session

If the first session was successful in breaking the rigid individual and relational patterns that fed the disorder, its significant effects can be verified in the second session. If so, a different atmosphere can typically be observed from the very start of the session, characterised by the different attitude of the parents – responsible and pleased – and by the different disposition of the girl – accommodating and open to communication.

For the young patient different elements represent an experience as reassuring as it is disruptive: the recovery of nourishment aimed at gradually regaining weight in connection with the concession to "forbidden" foods within the agreed dietary plan, and the reality of seeing her weight on the scale increasing only by the agreed amount. In addition, the fact that another person is taking responsibility for the situation makes her feel she has been relieved of the enormous burden she was carrying, which forced her to obsessively control her temptations.

The change of atmosphere is often so striking as to surprise even the most expert of therapists. However, we must be careful not to squander this achievement, since this change, however radical, must stabilise and then culminate in the actual healing of the patient.

For this reason, during the second session, after having discussed and analysed in detail the effects of the therapeutic intervention, *we congratulate the girl and her parents* for how successfully they have managed such a difficult trial, and we give them all the credit. *It is essential for the therapist to avoid exhibiting his or her own contribution*, because this would cause an immediate boycott of the therapy. At the same time, *enthusiasm is dampened* by declaring that, although this change is important, it represents just the first step.

28 Therapeutic treatment

We continue by saying that the road to healing is difficult and involves negotiating dangerous paths that require tenacity, determination, and acceptance of some painful stumbling, which it is important to tackle with even greater strength. In fact, a trap in the continuation of therapy is to rest on the laurels of the first impressive therapeutic change, as this makes us vulnerable to the unyielding pathology which will try to regain control. Anorexia is a delicate therapeutic challenge due to its resistance to change but, above all, to its relapses, which can be completely unexpected, as they may occur when the therapeutic process appears to be proceeding at its best.

For these reasons, usually from the second to the sixth session, *the therapeutic goal is to stay on course* and ensure that the girl regains, within the usual two months of treatment, the expected four–five kilograms, while getting used to her new dietary balance. Sometimes progression may stop or, conversely, accelerate too much; in both cases it is essential to *review with the family* what has produced this outcome and correct it. Beware: for the purpose of therapy, the second eventuality is actually more dangerous than the first. In fact, if the girl considers her therapist to have lost control of the healing process and of her reassuringly gradual weight gain, she loses confidence and falls back into the disorder. It is like saying, "if you drive too fast you will end up off the road" – that is, if the process of gaining weight and the accompanying healthy body shape become too evident because of a too-rapid transition, the frightened patient will reject them.

This stage of the therapy could appear less demanding and less challenging than the first stage in which more "dramatic" manoeuvres were put in place. Nevertheless, it is a delicate therapeutic process as it must provide stability and positive development to a quickly-achieved change.

To this end, the element which must be used to maximum advantage is the pleasure that has been regained and the one that is still to be discovered, not only concerning food but all the elements of a teenager's life. In each session, *some space is dedicated to creating evocative images of the taste of foods which were previously avoided*, and the patient is invited to make new "small explorations". The conversation focuses on how to combine foods to enhance their flavour, just as two chefs might talk about how to make their dishes tastier, while sharing suggestions both at a verbal and non-verbal level. As modern neurosciences teach, this activates the neural circuits of mirror neurons between patient and therapist, a powerful vehicle of influence that in this case creates positive feelings and a desire for that which was previously feared.

Third phase: from the sixth to the tenth session

If everything has gone according to plan, the girl will have regained a significant part of the lost weight and rediscovered the pleasure of food.

Furthermore, the family dynamics will be settling into a new hierarchical and relational balance. At this point, if not before, social relationships are resumed, and the patient once more begins to compare herself to others. What could seem natural is almost never natural in the case of anorexic disorders, and even resuming close interpersonal contacts with peers and the outside world represents an area of high risk. In most cases, perceived judgement by others, especially concerning her appearance, can be a source of suffering on which it is necessary to work carefully to avoid undermining what has been achieved up to this point.

It should be emphasised that, during the weight recovery and body desirability phase, the main source of distress for young female anorexic patients is not male judgement, but rather their own cruel comparison to other girls, who are always perceived as more beautiful, slim, and alluring. Generally, patients believe they are capable, but will minimise their abilities by declaring that they are only the result of a strenuous commitment. Thus, they experience a great sense of fragility. With such discrediting self-perceptions, it is easy to understand why the patient's relationship with the outside world appears threatening. Anorexia provides an effective and protective armour against this, too.

Clearly, this phase of the therapy *must focus on the girl's self-image*, on her relationship with others and on the acquisition of interpersonal skills, besides keeping the acquired physical and behavioural changes active and evolving. For this purpose, *the girl's perceived aesthetic defects are openly discussed with her*, without ever assuming the reassuring position typical of parents, who want to convince the daughter of her actual beauty. Instead, what she says is taken seriously, even when it appears absurd; corrective options are discussed with her by constantly offering concrete solutions (e. g., the use of fitness plans for the recovery of muscles). In short, just as the therapist took on the role of chef when talking about the pleasure of food, here he or she must play-act as a cosmetic surgeon, but *propose only achievable results* without use of scalpel, using only targeted motor activity, adequate nutrition, and aesthetic experiments aimed at the acceptance and improvement of the girl's self-perception. It is an *indirect way* to encourage weight gain through the girl's desire to make herself more attractive.

At the level of relationships, *the girl is led to "make others feel important"*, by showing interest in them through personal questions. It should be explained to her that this relational mode, consisting of focusing the attention on others, will make her appear desirable because everyone is pleased when feeling themselves the object of another person's interest. Moreover, this technique is useful in avoiding being subjected to other people's judgement, an area in which the girl is still too fragile. Usually this interpersonal communication strategy produces the desired effects almost immediately, giving her the feeling of being able to manage her relationship with her peers. This is an important thing for her because it relieves her from her fear of being unable to stand up to face others. At the same time, focusing on others during interpersonal exchanges yields the even greater effect of unlocking the obsessive self-control that is so typical of anorexia sufferers. This promotes not only her relationship with others but also her relationship with herself, making it less harsh and more flexible.

As illustrated, *we proceed to gradually dismantle* all the rigidities of the perceptive-reactive system typical of the anorexic pathology.

Fourth phase: from the tenth session onwards

If therapeutic intervention was fulfilled in the first three phases, what now remains is to build the new psychological equilibrium of the young woman, now freed from her anorexic disorder. Usually, at this stage we are faced with a patient who has completely or almost completely regained her weight and her physiological functions. In fact, the progression of half a kilogram per week allows patients to regain around 12 kilograms in about six months, which represents, if the case is not too serious, the achievement of the target weight. A longer time frame is necessary only in very critical cases, in which the weight to be recovered is even greater or the road to healing frequently goes downhill once the target weight is achieved. Therefore, this last part of the therapy *is mainly focused on the achievement of relational objectives and of the patient's adequate evaluation of her own resources, personal capabilities, and aesthetic qualities.* For this purpose, the space between sessions is expanded: usually appointments are set at a monthly frequency to allow the manifestation of experiences which the girl and the therapist will discuss one at a time. In this monthly treatment phase, which may be prolonged, *the role of the therapist is that of a supervisor* to whom the patient and her family relate in a process of growth after intensive care. At this point, there are no more therapeutic changes to achieve but, rather, a series of lessons that will become structured acquisitions. As we clarified elsewhere (Nardone & Balbi, 2015), an effective post-therapy process starts from the break of the pathological homeostasis and is realised through the construction of a new, healthy one. For this reason, eliminating the disorder and its symptoms is not enough; it is also necessary to cement all those acquisitions that brought about the girl's physical, behavioural, and self-perceptual changes into a new, self-maintaining psychological equilibrium.

Juvenile anorexia with *exercising*: therapeutic treatment

First phase: diagnosis-intervention

In the case of the *exercising* variant of juvenile anorexia, the first part of the session is performed in the same way as for the "pure" variant. However, once the physical exercise component has emerged from the discriminating dynamics as a relevant part of the disorder, we proceed by analysing whether this is the dominant element compared to restricted eating, or whether it is a secondary behaviour.

It is of fundamental importance to adapt the therapeutic intervention to the actual pathological reality by differentiating the intervention from the first session onwards. If the eating restriction has *exercising* as an additional symptom, the therapeutic *protocol* will be unchanged compared to that of pure juvenile anorexia, but it will include therapeutic *manoeuvres* designed to reduce compulsive movement to the point where this behaviour has been eliminated. Instead, if we are faced with a condition in which exercise predominates over food refusal as a way of avoiding weight gain or to facilitate weight loss, the therapeutic intervention will differ starting from the very first session. In the second case, we usually have a situation in which nutrition is not as restricted; however, the long walks or the frenetic sessions at the gym are so demanding that the calories lost will exceed those in the food consumed.

Therefore, even if the whole session is conducted using the same sequence of techniques, in the first case *the emphasis is placed on the fact that at least one of the parents will have to stay with their daughter for two hours after meals*. The girl needs to be engaged in various activities, for example talking, studying, or watching a movie or TV. This is to ensure that the compulsion to exercise within that time frame following meals is gently dissuaded; a very important part of the therapy. In the second case, in addition to this emphasis, from the first session onwards we will proceed *to negotiate the reduction of physical activity using a specific form of reframing* through an ad hoc prescription for this kind of problem. It is a variation of the illusion of response alternatives used for eating restriction: "Would you prefer to be locked up in a hospital room and forced to keep still, or will you agree to reduce your motor activity within the limits of healthy daily movement?" *These two alternatives will be accompanied by powerful evocative images*, similar to that of the "tube that blows you up like a balloon". For example, the image of being forced to use a wheelchair and forbidden to stand up. This practice is actually adopted in those forced admissions to hospital where the condition of the patient and her compulsion to exercise make it necessary. Persuasive negotiation can certainly be challenging, given the resistance of these patients to change. However, if the therapist persists and reaches an agreement with parents on the two alternatives, the girl will typically end up giving in. Rather than being forced to total immobility, she accepts to plan a drastic reduction of her motor activity to half an hour per day of aerobics in addition to a few minutes of stretching and strengthening exercises for the core muscles.

In these cases, *the therapist must demonstrate fitness trainer skills* by discussing with the girl, without fear of being contradicted, the correct level of daily motor activity needed to stay in shape while eating regularly and adequately. As well as being present at mealtimes and staying with their daughter for the following two hours, parents are given the added responsibility of assisting with, if not actively participating in, her training session. It is curious how often these therapies become a healthy nutrition and fitness programme for the whole family as, while helping the young daughter to free herself from her problem, they learn new and healthy habits.

The next phases of the therapy

The sequence of the therapeutic process follows the one explained above, since we are facing an anorexic juvenile disorder that, beyond the direct intervention on excessive movement, requires strategies and therapeutic stratagems aimed at deconstructing the pathological perceptive-reactive system of the patient.

In these cases it is important to notice that the girl's tendency to violate her therapy agreements is frequent, almost a rule. That is why the role played by the therapist is so crucial. During the sessions he or she gradually restructures the dysfunctional beliefs and perceptions concerning the excess of movement; the therapist turns the girl's image of the ideal of beauty from bodyweight to the harmony of the shape of the body. Equally important is the role played by the parents, who, besides being made aware of their responsibilities including "strategic blaming", should be supported to avoid demoralisation when faced with the often-exhausting difficulties and resistance of their daughter. However, *exercising* is both a physically and mentally stressful compulsive situation, and when the young anorexic patients manage to interrupt it, they experience an increased sense of well-being and feel as though a huge burden has been lifted. In this way therapeutic change, which was previously opposed, becomes embraced as a form of liberation from a prison. As happens in obsessive-compulsive disorders, a "catastrophic" type of therapeutic change (i.e., an almost immediate change) can be observed in a good percentage of cases. In the remaining cases, the compulsion is gradually eroded to the point where it collapses in on itself, achieving an "avalanche" effect.

Therefore, when *exercising* is predominant, the ultimate goal of the therapy is not only to help the girl regain a healthy weight, but also to regulate her motor activity. As with eating, exercise needs to become a pleasure rather than an obligation and must turn from a compulsive obsession into a pleasant and healthy activity.

Juvenile anorexia with *binge eating*: the treatment

As mentioned in the previous chapter, the variant characterised by alternating restricted eating and binge-eating, represents, along with *vomiting*, the evolution of juvenile anorexia when a girl loses control over her food intake. The fear of a total loss of control, and the consequent increasingly frequent binging, becomes the advantageous lever to use for therapeutic intervention. In fact, the *reframing of the "fear of fasting"*, which is the main therapeutic technique developed for this disorder, harnesses the fear of losing control over food intake to persuade the young anorexic to avoid fasting or skipping even a single meal, as this would trigger the inevitable binge.

> When a person sees themselves as fat or big, they think that the best solution for weight loss is fasting: the more I fast, the more I lose weight. Actually, you should start to be afraid of fasting, because each fast leads to a consequent binge. And if you fast for a period of time and then you binge-eat, you actually absorb even more calories, and therefore you do not lose weight. Start thinking of fasting as dangerous, because every time you fast you will end up subsequently binging, and this will cause you to put on, rather than lose, weight. I know that this is the only thing you can do and that you cannot manage not to do it, but think that, every time you try to restrict your diet to the point of skipping meals, you are actually setting yourself up for the next binge. Therefore, what you really should be afraid of is not the binge, which is an effect, but the fasting, which is the cause.

The reader should know that this type of treatment for *binge eating* has been empirically validated and has shown greater efficacy and persistence of results compared, through a controlled and randomised clinical trial, to cognitive-behavioural therapy (CBT), which is considered by many to be the gold standard (Jackson et al., 2018).

In similar cases, after having interrupted the pathological vicious circle of fasting and binging, *we try to ensure that the girl indulges in "small, pleasant food transgressions"*. This is done by using the same suggestive procedures described for pure anorexia (i.e., evoking the pleasurable sensations of tasting foods that the patients had forbidden themselves up until this point to gradually establish a food balance based on pleasure rather than control).

Most of the time, even in these situations, it is often necessary to regulate excessive motor activity on the part of the patients. For this purpose, we proceed by reframing the dysfunctional beliefs on exaggerated fitness, according to which patients apply the equation, "more *exercising* = more weight loss = more beauty". We focus attention on the power of excessive physical activity to stimulate hunger and its adverse effects on physical shape, for example because of the production of toxins and the induction of muscle mass catabolism. The girl is led to feel aversion to such behaviour and to favour a motor activity programme that instead allows her to maintain both her target weight and her psychophysical balance.

Although it may seem obvious, it is important to stress that the treatment of this variant of juvenile anorexia remains the same in its structure and sequence. However, some therapeutic stratagems are added, tailored to the dominant symptomatology (i.e., the alternation of restricted eating and binges). Once this dysfunctional pathological mode is extinguished, it is possible *to refocus the treatment on the disorder which is its root*. In fact, if we intervene only on the *binge eating* without resolving the anorexic pathology, the framework of the patient will evolve into either the most restrictive form of anorexia or into *vomiting* after eating. This is because the core of the pathology is still present and will tend to show itself in a different form or in a relapse with the same symptomatology.

Juvenile anorexia with *vomiting*: the treatment

Compulsive *vomiting* after eating represents the most dangerous and treatment-resistant development of the anorexic disorder. Similar to *binge eating*, it is characterised by an irrepressible compulsion to consume huge amounts of food which, in this case, are then thrown up. This behaviour tends to be perpetuated as a kind of rite, increasing in frequency as it gradually becomes more and more pleasant to the patient, until it becomes a compulsive pleasure that dominates the anorexic matrix. What is improperly defined as "anorexia nervosa" is in fact distinguishable from so-called "bulimia nervosa" as, in the former condition, the patient's low weight and fears of getting fat remain the cornerstones of the disorder. Therefore, in our therapeutic treatment it is necessary to intervene on these factors as well as to utilise techniques aimed at interrupting the irrepressible impulse to eat and then vomit. At the level of therapeutic planning, the same protocols for juvenile anorexia are applied, with some adaptations and with the addition of therapeutic practices developed specifically to address *vomiting*.

In this regard, it is important to note that, when the compulsion to vomit is in its initial phase, or when it is performed only after meals as a corrective practice driven by the fear of gaining weight, *the treatment advice given to parents that they should stay with their daughter for at least one hour after meals* represents an effective deterrent. Instead, if the compulsion is already strongly structured and/or characterised by an intrinsic sense of pleasure, the need or desire to vomit can make the young person at times violent and totally incapable of conforming to the constraints of a prescription. In other words, if the main crux of the pathology is still restricted eating, the parental supervision technique provides reassurance to the young anorexia sufferer both of the possibility of eating in moderation without over-eating, and of avoiding *vomiting*, which thus becomes no longer necessary. Conversely, if the *compulsion* to vomit has taken over as the pathological crux, it will overwhelm any attempt to control it. However, *the fear of getting fat is still, in these cases, an advantageous lever to be strategically used* to disrupt the cycle of over-eating and *vomiting*. In fact, the prescription of a time interval that must be left between binging and *vomiting*, which we will discuss in detail in the following pages, remains the main therapeutic technique (Dalle Grave, 2015; Nardone, 2003;

Nardone et al., 2005). In 25 years of work on this specific pathology, we have noted that *vomiting* has increasingly gained in popularity and is no longer considered something shameful that sufferers must hide.

In recent years, in fact, propagation and assimilation through social media has made *vomiting* the highest level of "evolution" for eating disorders, something to aspire towards as a devout follower of "ANA". At the level of therapy, this social acceptance has entirely nullified the effect of certain techniques that took advantage of the discomfort of making the acts of binging and *vomiting* apparent, unmistakable and even imposed upon and, paradoxically, accepted by one's family. In addition, the therapeutically disruptive prescriptions adopted in the nineties to induce embarrassment and shame are also now useless. These used to be proposed in a therapist's dialogue with patients and focused on bringing out and emphasising the erotic-transgressive connotation of this practice. Today, we could say that such prescriptions are "like water off a duck's back", since the very act of broadcasting everything on social media eliminates any form of social embarrassment, as is so typical of today's younger generation.

In addition, family dynamics have changed. Parents commonly now gripped by the fear of their daughter's retaliation will provide her with her requested food to binge and then vomit, just as in medieval tales of villagers who provided a dragon with nourishment to avoid being eaten themselves.

Because of all these evolutions, some therapeutic techniques developed in the past have now become obsolete. However, at the same time, these developments have validated an established fundamental therapeutic technique with a high rate of success for the therapy.

According to the insight of the early nineties, successful treatment of anorexia with *vomiting* entailed disconnecting pleasure from this rite, as well as taking advantage of the patient's fear of major weight gain. This understanding led to the elaboration of a technique that has now been widely validated.

The technique involves *prescribing*[1] *the young anorexic patient with complete freedom to eat and then vomit, as often as she wants, respecting only one simple rule: she must wait for an hour after each binge before she is allowed to vomit.*

If the patient agrees to put this suggestion into practice – and we will soon demonstrate the importance of persuasive communication to this end – the effect is twofold: the ritual changes from pleasant to unpleasant, and the amount of food consumed is spontaneously reduced due to the patient's fear of weight gain since *vomiting* is now delayed. Thus, this therapeutic manoeuvre works simultaneously on the compulsion to binge through leveraging the fear of getting fat, and on the compulsion to vomit by reducing the pleasure derived from the procedure. These therapeutic factors become even more powerful as treatment progresses because the time interval between the end of the act of eating and the beginning of the act of *vomiting* is increasingly extended, to the point where the disorder is in total remission.

Concerning the *therapeutic compliance* of patients (i.e., that is, the observance of and adherence to the prescription) it must be considered that, paradoxically, the most willing patients are those who have reached the highest levels of aggravation of the disorder and who are thus suffering from its disabling effects. Those still in the "pleasant experience" phase, not yet affected by the behaviour's simultaneous psychological, relational, and physiological drawbacks, show more resistance to the prescription. The more severe the disorder, the more effective and efficient the therapy.

However, as previously discussed, if the therapist has managed the first session effectively by evoking the fear of a forced hospital admission including "a tube that will blow you up like a balloon" and equally forced antiemetic treatment, even the most reluctant patients will respect and adhere to the therapy.

It should be stressed that, if the pattern and sequence of such compulsion is interrupted, the therapeutic effect is almost immediate, and the binging and *vomiting* stop very quickly. After this, the therapist can work on the other dimensions of the patient's juvenile anorexia, which will be easier to overcome once deprived of the rigid abstinence. In addition, interpersonal and social dynamics are constructively reorganised and experienced more rapidly, thanks to the fact that the rigidity towards pleasant sensations has now been relaxed. This "relaxation" is a difficult thing for the "pure" anorexia sufferers, as they are constantly worried about a loss of control. Meanwhile, for the girls affected by the variant of *vomiting*, it is a familiar experience that now allows them to relate to others without fearing intimacy. In fact, if the intervention is successful, the therapy of this variant is much shorter than for the primarily restrictive one.

An essential component in the treatment of anorexia with *vomiting* which should not be forgotten *is the emphasis on the role of communication and on the therapeutic relationship*. These young women, even more than "pure" anorexia patients, can be very challenging, provocative, and manipulative, and will manage their resistance to the therapy in an intelligent and strategic way. Therefore, the therapeutic dialogue becomes a "communicative duel" with no holds barred, where the patient, like an expert swordswoman, seeks the weak point of her opponent and does everything possible to catch them off guard and strike without mercy.

The therapist must be *able to skilfully manage communication and build a strong relationship with the patient, though this connection should never be rigid and directive* as this would be a demonstration of fragility. Instead, the relationship should be warm and gentle but also determined and orientated towards dismantling time and again the patient's disqualifying attacks or appealing manoeuvres to kindly lead her to capitulate. This is also an important lesson for parents who witness the therapist's verbal "duel" with their daughter until their daughter gives in and cooperates as she is no longer able to boycott the therapy at least for that single session.

Juvenile anorexia with *self-harming*: the treatment

It is important to remember that, for the purposes of therapeutic treatment, there are two types of *self-harm*: one with a *sedative function* that uses self-inflicted pain to distract from some negative event (e.g., a binge, a bad school mark, or an unrequited crush) and the other a *pleasing function* (i.e., the deliberate search for a kind of subtle pleasure). Often, when *self-harming* behaviour lasts a long time, the first type evolves into the second. However, at the level of the clinical intervention, it is important to evaluate the problem at its current stage in order to apply the appropriate therapy.

These two very different functions express themselves in a similar way at the level of their symptomatic manifestation. However, they require different therapeutic approaches because they are supported and nourished by different conditions, motivations, and psychological effects. The fact that these cases typically represent an evolutionary continuum of the disorder could erroneously lead the therapist to treat the underlying matrix. Nevertheless, the therapeutic techniques must *primarily* focus on the current functioning of the symptomatology instead of on its past function.

In the first case, *most of the time it is sufficient to successfully treat the eating disorder* in order to also bring about remission of the *self-harming* behaviour. In fact, treating the eating disorder eliminates the need for the "sedative effect" brought on by inducing deliberate physical pain in order to avoid feeling emotional pain. It is important to consider that, as we have repeatedly explained, the treatment of juvenile anorexia also involves solving relational problems and expressions of personal and interpersonal discomfort which may appear to be unrelated or indirectly related to the eating disorder. In this way, other forms of frustration that are at the basis of the *self-harm* behaviours also disappear.

In the second case, when the *self-harming* behaviour has become a pleasant ritual, the therapeutic intervention is the same as that successfully applied to obsessive–compulsive disorders based on pleasure: *the technique of the ritualisation of the ritual* (Nardone & Portelli, 2013). The girl is told to dedicate specific times during the day to performing the rite in a manner prescribed by the therapist, for example: "From now until the next session in two weeks' time, you must stand in front of the mirror every three hours and inflict your 'enjoyable torture' on yourself for two minutes …" This is a matter of making a symptomatic behaviour planned. This will remove from the behaviour that element of transgression that made it, among other things, so enjoyable. Moreover, the enforced routine transforms the patient's perception of the behaviour by gradually reducing its pleasure to the point where it becomes unpleasant.

This prescription is maintained for a few weeks, and the frequency of the rite is increasingly reduced, until it is extinguished entirely. However, patients will typically stop following the therapist's instructions by refusing to do something that has become a distasteful behaviour. This result *must be obtained in parallel with the therapeutic treatment of the eating disorder of which the self-harm is a part;* otherwise the risk of relapse is very high.

As illustrated above, the sedative function of *self-harming* behaviour is more frequent in restrictive anorexia where no pleasure is allowed, since pleasure is experienced as something from which to abstain, whatever its form, due to the fear of losing control. In contrast, the function of pleasant transgression can typically be found in the forms of anorexia with *vomiting* and *binge eating*, where it is accompanied by the pleasure of a compulsive loss of control over food.

Juvenile anorexia with *elimination:* the treatment

The use of laxatives and other methods to increase *elimination*, as well as powerful diuretics or various medications to lose weight or reduce the assimilation of ingested food, is not only one of the most frequent behaviours associated with anorexia but is also a form of addiction. The fact that this addiction is induced by the reiteration of behaviour and by the illusion of a desired effect makes it difficult to stop. The "explanatory lessons" of nutritionists, doctors, and sometimes even psychotherapists, who use reason and common sense to attempt to interrupt use and abuse of these products, have little effect. In the mind of the young anorexic their use represents a reassuring practice founded on an illusory belief but strengthened on a daily basis by the incessant marketing of the pharmaceuticals or the so-called "natural remedies" industries, which are amongst the richest consumer sectors in the world.

As with the aforementioned technique used to evoke the most primitive sensations related to the pleasure of food, treatment must be based on the most powerful, primitive, and paleo-encephalic perceptions and emotions to bring about an effective therapeutic change. A *suggestive and evocative reframing* to put in place during the dialogue with the patient is as follows:

> I know that using laxatives and diuretics is very reassuring for you … For this reason, I certainly cannot ask you to stop doing it. It would be useless to tell you that you could sustain serious intestinal damage, such as bowel occlusion and the narrowing of the anus, or other renal, cardiac, or neuromuscular consequences … However, it seems strange to me that someone, so clearly intelligent and studious as you has missed the fact that these are largely ineffective, since the absorption of food takes place in the small intestine while these act on the large intestine. So, what appears reassuring to you actually ends up creating what scares you … Laxatives lead to *meteorism*, which is when there is a lot of gas in one's abdomen, making the stomach bloated, distended, and stick out … There are several methods that you could use to control your weight, have a flat stomach, and look beautiful. Of course, you would have to let yourself be guided …

Usually, after such a persuasive argument, which leverages a slight to the patient's intelligence and their fear of the effects of laxative abuse, patients agree to *start gradually reducing the use of substances and practices that facilitate elimination, until they cease use altogether.*

As seen, nothing is forced; we use only the evocative and persuasive power of therapeutic dialogue that was strategically built to create aversion towards that which was previously desired.

Juvenile anorexia with *substance abuse*: the treatment

The therapeutic intervention for juvenile anorexia complicated by the abuse of chemicals involves two procedures: the predominantly psychological treatment described in the preceding pages and physiological detoxification from the effects of dependency and addiction.

This strategy applies to both the use of illegal drugs and the abuse of certain types of medicine. In fact, at our treatment centre in Arezzo we employ a neurologist who is an expert in detoxification from drugs and medicines and whose intervention proceeds in parallel with the psychotherapy. In this way, the patient and her family can be reassured that both features of the pathology are treated with a single therapeutic approach. Additionally, as experts in the field understand, an approach focused on only a single aspect of the disorder would have numerous limitations and would not produce the positive results that are achieved with integrated treatment.

Psychological substance addiction is no less powerful than physiological addiction and requires therapeutic techniques that allow the young female to free herself from the chains that imprison her. However, in our experience, if the eating disorder therapy works well and if the rigid patterns begin to be disrupted in the very first sessions, the girl will be more willing to follow the directives for gradually reducing the *substance abuse*. This is particularly true if these substances were part of the attempted anorexic solutions used by the girl to manage her body size and nutrition. Therefore, it is also essential in such cases to bring about therapeutic change in relation to anorexia; in this way, the use and abuse of substances is deprived of its function. The remaining addiction will be gradually overcome with the patient's active collaboration.

Multi-symptomatic juvenile anorexia and/or borderline personality disorder: the treatment

Many authors have highlighted the fact that when anorexia lasts for a long time and expresses itself with different serious symptoms that are either expressed simultaneously or that alternate over the years, the risk of developing a borderline personality disorder is very high. Considering the acceleration of the processes exacerbating anorexic pathology in juveniles, the number of patients at risk, or that already have a borderline pathology, is increasing. This further complicates the job of the therapist, considering that treating juvenile anorexia is already in itself a complex process. In such cases, an oscillation between different symptomatic modes represents the rule, not the exception, and the incidence of relapses after therapeutic improvements are so frequent as to be almost predicable.

It is as though these patients are walking a tightrope without a stabiliser; they are unstable before they fall, and they return to the tightrope only to sway again until the next fall. *These patients need to obtain a balancing bar*, and to limit their oscillations to a range that can be controlled. In reality, they have devastated personalities, are unable to maintain regularity in behaviours and thoughts, and are deeply emotionally unstable. Therefore, *in addition to dealing with the eating disorder, the therapy must focus on creating a basic psychological balance* on which the foundations of a stable and integrated personality can gradually be built.

At first, it is the therapist who acts as a stabilising bar for the incapable tightrope walker; that is, *the therapist must be the fundamental reference point* for the young patient who must feel that she can trust him or her. Then, security and psychological balance will be built by working simultaneously on behaviours, emotions, and thought processes related both to personal and interpersonal dynamics. This balance is necessary in order to avoid regressing to a continuous oscillation between falls and recovery attempts.

In other words, *the role of the therapist must be that of a captain who takes the helm of the girl's life and teaches her to manoeuvre step by step*, even in the most difficult situations.

The personality of the therapist is clearly important in these cases; as reported by most experts, the therapist must be charismatic as well as able to make patients feel guided, protected, and encouraged to improve their own skills which are usually significant (Cotugno & Benedetto, 1995; Loriedo, 2013; Petrini et al., 2012). Otherwise, the therapist is likely to become hostage to patients who are very good at forging toxic and manipulative connections.

Therefore, the therapeutic relationship should move between intimacy and detachment, warmth and distance, confidence and diffidence, without ever allowing the patient to take control. Unsurprisingly, these are the cases in which therapists are most frequently beguiled by patients, thus thwarting the possibility of positive therapeutic outcomes.

Most of the time, parents are totally unable to manage their daughter and are willing to pass off the role of guide to the therapist, on whom they also rely. It is precisely this typical surrender by the parents that allows the therapist to provide specific behavioural instructions that are generally humbly accepted and strictly observed. The important thing is *to avoid asking the parents what they are emotionally unable to do*; otherwise, if we force them to face their inability, we will lose their trust in us. Like their daughter, they often also need to learn how to take the helm and cannot be given free rein without the direct assistance of an expert.

In general, the therapeutic objective with a borderline personality disorder, even more so if it is associated with an eating disorder, is to stay on course without surrendering to the currents and winds that life inevitably places along the way. In the words of expert Piero Petrini (2012), these young women are "stable in instability and unstable in stability" and must be made stable in stability.

Moreover, several important historical figures are known to have had well-stabilised borderline personalities; that is to say that they each learned the acrobatic art of walking the tightrope while staying balanced by virtue of a stabilising bar that they were able to build and beautifully handle.

The treatment of juvenile anorexia: summarise to redefine

To conclude the chapter, we consider it important to summarise some essential points that highlight the rigour and flexibility of this type of therapeutic intervention. Moreover, we will stress its compliance to the international guidelines for the treatment of juvenile anorexia, and the techniques that allow the therapy to increase its effectiveness and efficiency.

The therapy starts with a session of high therapeutic impact, aimed at undermining the pathological patterns that support and nourish the juvenile anorexic disorder.

At first, this is realised at the level of family dynamics: parents are empowered and guided to modify their problematic modes of managing their daughter's disorder. In this way, the young patient finds herself in a situation where a change is inevitable, but where she may choose the more acceptable, less strenuous, and least dangerous way in which to bring it about.

Afterwards, perceptions and emotions related to the desire for food and aversion to fasting are evoked in the patient, by using suggestive-hypnotic techniques. At this point, we negotiate with her a nutrition programme that appears both reassuring and pleasant.

These steps are then concreted in a family action plan whereby parents are further empowered in assisting their daughter during and after meals.

Depending on the symptomatic variants, specific *ad hoc* therapeutic manoeuvres are added to the *"invariant session"*.

This represents the key part of the therapeutic treatment; in fact, if performed successfully, it is possible to observe a rapid change which is the result of a session studied in every detail. The session is studied both from the point of view of the strategy and the applied stratagems, and from that of the suggestive-hypnotic communication and the assertive relationship.

The latter is resolute and decisive but, at the same time, emotionally warm and reassuring (Nardone & Salvini, 2004; Nardone & Watzlawick, 1993; Watzlawick & Nardone, 2001).

The remainder of the therapeutic process, while no less important than the first session, is determined by its effects. This is true to the point that, until the emotional corrective experience[2] (Alexander, 1946) that breaks the pathological balance has been produced, the healing process cannot start. The reader should understand that the strategically induced therapeutic change is not a random event resulting from a non-specific clinical session unfocused on the pathology, as is often claimed should be used in long-term therapies (Stern, 2004). When it comes to high-risk pathologies which frequently become chronic, we believe that the first intervention should be aimed at promptly interrupting the pathological dynamics of food and body management. If the therapy does not produce positive results in a short time, the risks favour the disorder becoming chronic.

As stated, this type of treatment is precisely tailored to the needs of the problem and to the specific features of the person in treatment by differentiating the techniques based on the specific pathological variant. Even when these techniques are rigorously replicated, they will differ in the language and type of therapeutic relationship used, always adapting to the unique characteristics of each patient and family system. Indeed, a fundamental aspect of the strategic approach to psychotherapy is the coexistence of *regularity and originality* in the therapeutic intervention.

Another important element of this model of treatment is the focus, from the very first session onwards, on the antagonist nature of anorexic abstinence. Pleasure is the primal feeling – the emotion which nobody can resist; pleasure is the very feeling anorexia would like to eradicate by means of abstinence. It is pleasure that represents the advantageous lever to unhinge the lock of the "anorexic strongbox". Even Saint Augustine, who could never be accused of practicing hedonism, cautioned that "no one can live without pleasure".

Pleasure is first evoked suggestively and the patient experiences it mentally in a reassuring way; it is then gradually nurtured and amplified throughout the therapeutic process, so that it becomes something that the patient can allow herself to feel without fear of losing control.

When the young woman starts eating again and regains weight, and the most disabling symptomatic elements are in remission, the therapy proceeds with the construction of a new psychological balance characterised by perceptual, emotional, behavioural, and cognitive shifts that promote her well-being. In juvenile anorexia, differential psychological and relational issues need to be taken into account, as these are peculiar to puberty and adolescence. Such patients need to be accompanied in their path of growth, bearing in mind that they often shift between the desire for independence, affirmation, and autonomy, and the need for protection associated with the fear of growing up. Therefore, the beginning of a school year or its end, the entry into the world of work, the development of an emotionally significant relationship, and the separation from parents or other family ties are the main areas of investigation since these are the potential sources of critical situations.

The consolidation phase is a fundamental part of a good therapeutic outcome and can last for a long time. However, appointments are spaced out and organised in a type of long-term follow-up that can continue for years. For many of these patients the therapist must become a reference point, able to provide the necessary tools and security for managing situations that are frightening or stressful, until the attainment of complete autonomy. In this way, it is possible to guarantee the lowest possible risk of relapse or development of other replacement pathologies in place of the anorexia.

Notes

1 "From now until our next meeting, I suggest you do this experiment. Whenever you feel the impetus to eat and then vomit, you can indulge in it by binge-eating, binge-eating to the point where you feel full and want to throw up everything you have gulped down. At that point, you must stop and wait for an hour, without eating, drinking, or anything else. Exactly after one hour, you may go and throw up. I know it will be difficult but doing this will be the first important step towards taking control of the situation and avoiding being forever enthralled."
2 This expression was introduced by Alexander in 1946 to indicate those concrete emotional experiences that allow the patient to "correct" the traumatic experience of previous negative experiences. According to the prominent author, the most significant and lasting changes take place by virtue of real experiences lived by the patient in the present, in their relationship with the therapist, or in their daily life, which are capable of undermining the effect of the past events. This concept has been taken up and extended by the brief strategic approach where it has become one of the main cornerstones of the therapeutic process. This perceptual-emotional experience of change can be induced both within the therapeutic session, for example, thanks to the use of the strategic dialogue, and between sessions, thanks to the use of prescriptions to be put in place in the patient's everyday life (Nardone & Salvini, 2019).

Chapter 5

Juvenile anorexia: the effective therapy

Giorgio Nardone, Elisa Valteroni, Gianluca Castelnuovo

Introduction

For more than four decades, studies on therapies for mental anorexia have addressed the disorder in broad terms without any differentiation between adult anorexic sufferers and those in childhood and adolescence. Only in the last decade, due to the spread of the disorder at an earlier age, has systematic research on its treatment been carried out. Although mental anorexia – without distinguishing between adult patients and pubescent adolescents – has received more attention than juvenile anorexia, the effectiveness of the therapies has been little investigated. The prestigious magazine *Lancet* recently published a review of studies conducted on eating disorders according to internationally recognised methodological criteria. The article reports that, while there are over 50 studies on bulimia nervosa, the studies in the field of mental anorexia comprise only little more than a fifth. In this type of research, the statistical experimental design, although rigorous, is based on a small group of patients that was compared with an equally small control group. However, if we also consider the international literature and purely clinical empirical studies – certainly less rigorous but implemented on broader sample sizes and with long-term follow-ups concerning therapy outcomes – it is possible to identify the most suitable treatment for this disorder.

Castelnuovo (2019), who oversaw the review on the effectiveness of psychotherapies in the *International Dictionary of Psychotherapy*, indicated the forms of psychotherapy that have demonstrated a significant efficacy for eating disorders: systemic-family psychotherapy (especially for anorexia), cognitive-behavioural psychotherapy (especially for bulimia nervosa and *binge eating*), brief strategic psychotherapy (especially for anorexia, *binge eating,* and *vomiting*), and finally, integrative psychotherapy (exclusively for bulimia).

Interestingly, these four types of intervention clearly have some elements in common. This is true in particular for systemic-family therapy and brief strategic therapy (BST) as they share theoretical and operational assumptions. If we distinguish juvenile anorexia from adult anorexia, as would be appropriate according to the most recent research, the indicators of the most effective therapy and the fundamental therapeutic factors emerge even more clearly.

Recently, the Royal Australian and New Zealand College of Psychiatrists (RANZCP, 2014) published its guidelines for the treatment of eating disorders, and juvenile anorexia is finally considered as distinct from adult anorexia in relation to treatment. The scientific evidence clearly shows that the most suitable therapy for this type of disorder is a *family-based* therapy with a systemic-strategic approach (Ball & Mitchell, 2004; Eisler et al., 2000; Le Grange et al., 2010; Lock, 2011; Robin et al., 1994; Russell et al., 1987 1987). From the very first session, this therapy focuses on producing changes in the patients' diet and on increasing their weight; whereas specific therapeutic techniques are suitable for other symptoms such as *vomiting* and *exercising*. The positive prognostic factor appears to be a weight gain of two kilograms in four weeks and a noticeable change in the eating style of the patient (Le Grange et al., 2010; Lock, 2011). A lot of emphasis is placed on parents' empowerment with respect to their therapeutic role (Le Grange, 2004; Le Grange et al., 2003; Le Grange & Lock, 2005; Lock, 2002). However, this does not mean that all the sessions should be conducted in the presence of the entire family. In fact, the alternation between individual and family meetings within the same session is definitely to be preferred for juvenile anorexia associated with other disabling symptoms (*vomiting, exercising, binge eating,* purging, and *substance abuse*).

Another important result provided by these systematic studies is the recognition that the first line of treatment for juvenile anorexia should not involve hospitalisation. Hospitalisation is necessary only in cases where there is a real risk of death or irreversible health damage and should be of limited duration when necessary. The outpatient psychotherapeutic treatment consisting of weekly or bi-weekly sessions is the most effective treatment. Another relevant consideration concerns the lack of utility of psychopharmacological treatments; the latest research does not show a significant therapeutic rationale regarding the use of medications for people with anorexia (Hay et al., 2014; Kearns et al., 2003; Steffen et al., 2007).

With regard to psychotherapy, a relevant fact is that only *ad hoc* models work with this type of disorder. That is, models that are centred both on the rapid modification of factors feeding the disorder and on the elimination of the restrictive eating symptomatology. Instead, generic psychotherapies not focused on the disorder appear to be ineffective and may even allow the disorder to become a chronic condition (Dalle Grave, 2015; Lock & Couturier, 2009).

However, after having unlocked the restrictive eating behaviour, it is important for the therapy to take into consideration all the other issues in the life of the young patient to ensure the effectiveness of the treatment. This means that the therapy is not only focused on food and weight, but also deals with the development of a healthy psychological balance and interpersonal and social skills and, at the same time, fosters the development of a functional family dynamic.

In confirmation of this, for any readers who still have doubts, RANZCP guidelines (2014) reported nine specific randomised clinical trials conducted exclusively on juvenile anorexia. An additional 12 studies on anorexia included a specific section for juvenile anorexia. More recently, the contributions by Marcelle Barruco Costa and Tamara Melnik (2016), Glenn Waller (2016) and Daniel Le Grange (2016) confirmed such empirical findings.

Therefore, it is clear that the results of research on the effectiveness of such treatments confirm the validity of the type of treatment exposed thus far, that is to say, a form of brief strategic and systemic therapy studied ad hoc for juvenile anorexia. This therapy follows the indications coming from the studies on this subject, in association with other specific therapeutic techniques developed in the last decade in the clinical work on the juvenile anorexic disorder and subjected to research-intervention experimentation (Nardone, 2003; Nardone & Selekman, 2011; Nardone et al., 2005).

Effectiveness and efficiency of the brief strategic therapy at the Strategic Therapy Centre (STC) in Arezzo

In accordance with the research history of the Palo Alto School, our research has focused mainly on strategies and therapeutic stratagems that can quickly resolve the most common and disabling psychopathologies. To this end, our method has been that of clinical research-intervention (i.e., the direct experimentation of techniques and their refinement on large numbers of patients with the help of a system which allows us to record and review the therapeutic sessions). Measurement[1] of therapy outcomes was agreed with patients using a 0 to 10 scale and was performed both at the end of the therapy and during a one-year follow-up session. This method allowed us to build over 30 brief strategic treatment protocols for different forms of psychological and behavioural pathology. The percentages of positive therapeutic outcomes are in many cases superior to those of other forms of treatment (Nardone, 1993, 2016; Nardone & Portelli, 2005, 2013; Nardone & Selekman, 2011; Nardone & Watzlawick, 2005; Nardone et al., 2005).

Over the last 15 years, we have conducted quantitative research on efficacy and efficiency of therapies along with studies that are essentially qualitative, so as to satisfy the most recent academic-scientific criteria for the evaluation of evidence of therapeutic efficacy and to compare our model of treatment with other approaches on the international scene. We have repeatedly discussed (Nardone & Salvini, 2019) how such studies may often seem arbitrary, reductive, and not very significant to us with regard to the impact on patients' real possibilities of healing. Indeed, such research is mostly carried out on a small and very selective number of patients that at times is not truly representative of the clinical population, thus creating problems for generalising treatments outside the "laboratories" where many variables are controlled or weighted. Moreover, in such experimental contexts, the validity of a treatment is frequently defined by the different statistical significance tests used, ignoring clinical significance, which is not merely a question of numbers.

A Randomised Controlled Trial (RCT) (Castelnuovo et al., 2010; Jackson et al., 2018), compared the results of BST and CBT on patients with a *binge eating* disorder and comorbid obesity. The results showed that BST was statistically and clinically superior in reducing binge frequency, weight, and clinical symptomatology and the maintenance of these results over time compared to CBT, which is typically considered to be the *gold standard* for the treatment of eating disorders. A more recent article (Pietrabissa et al., 2019) shows the empirical evidence of the effectiveness of BST as a treatment for eating disorders.

Other studies of this type, specifically conducted on juvenile anorexia, confirm these data. Amongst these, RCTs conducted by Robin (1994, 1999) and Ball and Mitchell (2004), comparing BST to other forms of psychotherapy, including CBT, also concluded that BST was superior.

A series of studies have adopted pre- and post-treatment evaluations by external evaluators (e. g., psychiatrists, independent psychotherapists, and "pure" researchers not involved in the studies). These experts compared the patients' initial condition with that at the end of the therapy by means of internationally shared and standardised diagnostic techniques (Nardone et al., 2013; Nardone & Barbieri Brook, 2010). Specific attention was paid to external validity (i.e., the generalisability of results in different cultural contexts), which is why the analyses were performed in the United States, Russia, Mexico, Colombia, Spain, France, Belgium, Austria, the Netherlands, and Romania, with outcome percentages very similar to those obtained in Italy.

With regard to the juvenile anorexia treatment approach described, an evaluation study was performed with the usual research-intervention methodology[2] with the help of independent and well-trained external observers. The sample consisted of 228 cases diagnosed with juvenile anorexia according to international diagnostic criteria. The age of the participants ranged between 12 and 19. Participants came from various regions of Italy, with the exception of eight international cases, of which four were European, two North American and two South American. All patients were treated by Giorgio Nardone and his collaborators (i.e., students of the Postgraduate School of Brief Strategic Therapy in Arezzo), between 2010 and 2016. In each case, data were collected before therapy began and 6 and 12 months after the conclusion of therapy (most of these follow-ups were extended up to two years after the therapeutic outcome) from patients and their parents to evaluate the persistence of the changes made by the patient.

In terms of the results, 41 cases (18%) dropped out of the therapy, 21 of these after the first session, and 20 between the first and the tenth session. We interpreted these dropout cases as "therapeutic failure", even though the clinical literature recommends disregarding early drop-outs in the evaluative analysis. In our case, however, given the importance of the first session not only for its diagnostic value but, above all, for its therapeutic intervention value, this result was interpreted as a victory of resistance to change over our attempt to unlock the pathological situation. In total, 187 cases (82%) were successfully treated, with the treatment lasting from a minimum of five sessions to a maximum of 31 sessions, over a time frame of 6 to 12 months. The majority of cases required between 10 and 20 sessions, and only in about a fifth of the cases did treatment last fewer than ten sessions or more than 20.

As the data show, on an extended sample of treated participants, the therapeutic outcomes of the advanced BST model for juvenile anorexia are significantly higher in terms of both efficacy and efficiency compared to other forms of psychotherapy. Furthermore, by replicating the results of other studies conducted in previous decades, these conclusions demonstrate the validity of this theoretical-applied model that continuously evolves based on the empirical-experimental research in this field, adapting the therapeutic strategies to the transformation of psychopathologies over time.

To use the words of George Lichtenberg: "the best proof of a theory is in its application".

Gianluca Castelnuovo is a psychologist, psychotherapist, and Associate Professor in Clinical Psychology at the Faculty of Psychology of the Catholic University of Milan. He is a researcher and clinician at the Service and Laboratory of Clinical Psychology of the IRCCS (Scientific Institute for Research, Hospitalization and Healthcare) Italian Auxological Institute. He is also a Member of the Board of the Italian Society of Eating Disorders (SIS-DCA).

Notes

1 The success of a therapy is established on the basis of the remission of the disabling symptoms and the recovery of the perception of psychological well-being confirmed by significant improvements in all areas of the everyday life of the patient.
2 The reader should know that carrying out an efficacy study of treatments that includes a control group of untreated patients in addition to the experimental group under treatment is neither feasible nor ethical for the treatment of anorexia. This is due to the fact that untreated participants are subjected to diagnostic measurements and waiting for a possible treatment, which leads to positive or negative changes in their condition. Furthermore, it is certainly unethical to avoid treating patients who suffer from a disabling and dangerous condition such as anorexia for the sole purpose of meeting the control group criterion required by rigorous standardised research.

Appendix

The appendix provides the transcripts of the therapy sessions of two clinical cases treated at the Strategic Therapy Centre of Arezzo. The first case concerns the treatment of a 15-year-old girl with pure anorexia. The full transcripts of the therapy sessions up to the unblocking of the pathological pattern of the patients are provided, with the addition of a summary of the following phases of the therapy until its conclusion. The second case is an example of very brief therapy for juvenile anorexic disorder. For this case, the complete transcripts of the entire therapeutic process, which consisted of ten sessions, including the first follow-up after three months are provided. The transcripts are accompanied by the authors' notes to guide the reader into the understanding of the therapeutic steps that progressively lead the young patients towards change.

Case I

This is a case of a 15-year-old girl with pure anorexia. She was already involved in a traditional para-hospital treatment programme for eating disorders when she came to the Strategic Therapy Centre of Arezzo accompanied by her mother, who requested an urgent appointment due to her daughter's resistance to the treatment programme. A complete transcript of the first five sessions is given below. During these sessions, the pathological perceptive-reactive system of the young patient is unlocked, together with the introduction of a more varied, healthy, and pleasant eating regime, and initial weight recovery. In addition, other important objectives that were achieved and maintained in the subsequent and concluding phases of therapy will be briefly described.

T: Therapist; CT: Co-therapist; P: Patient; M: Mother; F: Father

First session

T: Good evening, please have a seat. I have done my best to see you as soon as possible. So, what's the problem?

M: P. has had an anorexia disorder for several months. – *Operational definition of the problem* –
T: Just a few months ... Hmm. Could you describe it exactly in all its phases?
M: An alarm bell rang in my head because she wasn't getting her period, not since October 2007, but at first ... given her age ... Two or three months have passed like this. Around the beginning of the year we talked to our doctor and then to a psychologist. They told us that they couldn't solve the problem because she seemed very severe already, because she lost several kilograms: ten since she weighed herself a few months earlier, from October 2007 to January, from 53 to 44 kilograms. Currently I don't know her exact weight. However, they told us that we should speak to the hospital medical team [...]
T: Does this mean that the psychologist [...] had been seeing her for a while?
M: No, only one session as suggested by the psychologist herself [...] Only that session, in which she first had a conversation with my daughter alone, then with us parents. Then, she told me that she didn't consider herself suitable to help P. because she only works on mental processes, while she felt that here there was also a physical, not just psychological, issue. So, she told us to contact the team of [...] There they gave us an appointment for Thursday the 10th. There was this session with the doctor [...] Two hours with the three of us all together, P. and us two parents. She was very direct and told her that this is anorexia nervosa and that P. would have to undergo some tests immediately. Today she did the ECG to see if her internal organs have suffered any damage. This morning she did the ECG. The nurse, while she was doing it, said that her heartbeat is very weak. So now, after receiving this news from the doctor [...] P. fell into a crisis because she says: "I'm sick, I'm not normal anymore". Then the doctor immediately made her stop any physical activity, because she used to play volleyball. And she is desperate because she doesn't feel normal anymore. The same is true for us because we have started to get anxious and afraid that there's something wrong on a physical level that she has actually suffered some physical damage.
T: Ok, what is the team's intervention programme?
M: We're supposed to go there on Tuesday. She's against it. They will examine her to evaluate her physical state and, if needs be, she will be treated in the partial hospitalisation programme for therapeutic rehabilitation.
T: [to P.]: And you got scared ...
P: Yes.
T: But what is the thing that scares you the most: the fact that you might be sick, as they say, or the fact that someone wants to intervene to make you gain weight?[1] – *Discerning strategic question* –
P: More than anything else, the fact that because I've stopped physical activity all my friends will know about it. I feel like I'm not normal like I was before.

T: Is this the thing that scares you the most?
P: Yes.
T: Hmm, you're right. Do you see any way out of this situation?
P: Well, right now, a way out seems very difficult.
T: Hmm, what if I said that if you regain your weight quickly, you could resume all your activities, and nobody would notice anything. Or is that asking too much of you? – *Discerning strategic question* –
P: It's difficult.
T: Ah ... let's go back to the previous question: what is it that scares you the most?
P: Regaining weight.
T: Ok, fine. But is it clear that, if you want to stay like this, everyone will know that you have a problem? Also, P., do you think that nobody has noticed?
P: They have noticed.
T: If a girl like you, 15 years old, loses ten kilograms and reaches a weight of 40 kilograms, then everyone can see it. You're walking around with it written on your forehead: "anorexia". – *Restructuring* –

So this seems like a false problem, let me tell you, it's painful but it's the effect of the other problem, it's not the main problem. Ok ... I'll ask you an even more direct question: are you willing to tackle this problem and solve it, in the full knowledge that you will need to gain weight until your reach a healthy weight, which will also correspond to the return of your menstrual cycle, or do you think you're okay at the moment? – *Discerning strategic question* –

P: Let's say that I would like to stay like this, but I can't because I'm so bad, but I'd like to stay like this.
T: Ok, I appreciate your honesty. You're telling me, "A very strong part of my mind is telling me that I'm fine like this, stay this way". The other, weaker part, feeble but reasonable, is saying that you can't stay like this because you're so sick. – *Restructuring paraphrase* –
P: Yes.
T: So, right now do you feel ready to collaborate and work together to get back to being as beautiful as you can be, or do you feel uncooperative? – *Discerning strategic question* –
P: Not very collaborative.
T: Well ... then to be very clear I think that the partial hospitalisation program and the drip-feed are the only thing you can do. If, instead, you were collaborative in working on nutrition and on your self-image in a different way, then those could be avoided ... I'm not asking you for an answer right away, I'm just asking you to consider if you like the idea of going to a hospital or a clinic where they'll drip-feed you. And if that

doesn't work then they'll put a tube in your nose and force-feed you until you blow up like a balloon, so over a short space of time they'd be able to make you gain several kilograms. Or, if you'd prefer to increase your weight by eating gradually ... There are no alternatives. Be careful, because your parents, even if they wanted to accommodate you, can't do anything because you are not of age, so they are your legal guardians and they have parental responsibility and a legal duty to protect your health. You can decide whether to gain weight in the hospital out of your own control and get yourself blown up quickly like a balloon, or gradually within your control by deciding together what to eat. What's on your mind right now?[2] – *Question with illusion of response alternative with analogical image of a balloon* –

P: The fear of gaining weight, but also the desire to go back to how things were before. But I don't want to go to the partial hospitalisation program.

T: I completely agree with you, but you must deserve that. Let's try to think about how to avoid that, how to deserve it ... But this means that you will need to be collaborative. – *Use of communicative ambivalence to stimulate functional behaviour* –

P: Yes, yes [*she half smiles*].

T: Good. Then, can you tell me what your current daily nutrition is, from the time you wake up in the morning to the time you go to sleep at night? – *Investigation on daily nutrition* –

P: In the morning when I get up I have a glass of fruit juice and two cookies. Then, at school, only recently because I'd stopped earlier, but lately I have iced tea and a sandwich. Then when I go home for lunch, I have more or less a first and second course, but with reduced portions. Then in the afternoon a yogurt or a fruit juice and for dinner a piece of pizza or soup with flatbread.

M: That's only recently though, because in the meantime the doctor sent us to a dietitian who wrote down this diet that consists of eating what she just described. In fact, she didn't have any breakfast in the morning for months because she said she was sick, and she wasn't even eating the sandwich at school. So, let's say she was having lunch and dinner. Then she started this diet a couple of months ago. I have noticed one thing, and I don't know if it's serious, but she has this excess saliva that she spits into paper tissues.

T: Are you sure it's saliva?

M: Well, she uses lots of tissues and they're always full.

T: This is a different thing and it's the reason why she keeps losing weight.[3] – *Redefinition of the patient's pathological behaviour: she does not swallow the food, she spits it out, therefore she continues to lose weight* –

T: [Speaking to P.] Then you spit out a lot of it, am I right? It's not saliva in the tissue, is it? You know, I have to tell you that I recognise your problem and have been working with it for a long time. Usually when girls are

forced to eat they learn to spit out the food or to vomit. It's pretty clear that if you actually were eating what you said you're eating, then you wouldn't still be losing weight. In fact, you would have already started to gain weight.
M: Even though she's been exercising up until yesterday? She was doing a lot.
T: What do you mean by "a lot"?
M: Volleyball four times a week.
T: How many hours?
M: Two hours a day.
T: What does this mean? Is this a lot?
M: Yes.
T: Madam, true sufferers of anorexia exercise eight hours a day. [Speaking to P.] So, if you decide to start eating without spitting out your food, we could also resume your physical activity soon without any major problems, and this would help you to recover better instead of being inactive. But you must decide for yourself: you can be blown up like a balloon with a tube, or you can avoid this by respecting certain conditions ... – *Use of the pleasure of performing motor activity to stimulate functional nutritional behaviour* –
P: I don't want to go there.
T: If you were sure you wouldn't get fat, what would be the foods you'd like best? Would you prefer sweet or savoury food? Soft or crunchy food? Cold or hot dishes? – *Evoking the pleasure of dreaded foods* –
P: Crunchy pizza with lots of mozzarella, red tomato, and some fragrant basil leaves is my favourite dish ... the sandwiches they make at school with smoked ham, mushroom sauce or truffles are delicious, and chocolate biscuits ... But I like a little bit of everything, that's the problem ... Pasta with ragu, meat, and soups ... I would love them ...
T: So, since the diet plan that they gave you contains exactly what you like the most, we would like you to eat exactly what you have been told. You, madam [speaking to the mother] simply have to avoid pushing her to do it. You should prepare everything for her and you should observe, but you must absolutely avoid talking about it in the family, pushing her, saying: "eat"; you just have to give her the food. It is her responsibility: if she wants to end up in hospital and be blown up like a balloon, the problem is hers. – *Prescriptions, food indications, conspiracy of silence, and observation without family interference* –
M: But do I have to weigh out the amounts or not?
T: We weigh with our eyes; never make the weight of food into an obsession. You simply have to give her the planned foods, and then it's her problem if she eats them or not. You know, P., that either you will recover your weight in a certain way or there will be the tube and you'll be blown up like a balloon, and it's clear that if you keep spitting out food and vomiting it's the same thing. [Speaking to the parents] You'll go to the medical

examination, so we will have a measure of everything. Tuesday is three days from now, so let's see what she does. If your daughter starts eating again, she can tell the doctors and you will go to a check-up after a month. However, it is useful to have a measure, a check, a sort of sword of Damocles, as a reminder: that unwanted possibility is always there. That's helpful. All right? I would like to see you next Thursday and we will go over what has happened then.

M: Do I need to bring you the results, Professor?

T: Yes, bring them with you. [Speaking to P.] So, I'll see you on Thursday and we'll see then if you want the tube or if you want to do this in a different way, okay?

P: Yes.

As we can see from this transcription, the first session was structured to follow, as described in the text, all the phases of the therapeutic protocol for juvenile anorexia. In the first part of the session, through the use of discerning strategic questions, the therapist assesses the rigidity and pervasiveness of the patient's perceptive-reactive anorexic system and investigates motivation for change and collaboration. In fact, if the girl had been immediately ready to regain weight, eliciting the fear of impending forced-feeding at the hospital or clinic would not have been necessary.

Once a collaborative base, on which to work directly with the patient and parents, is established the nutrition plan indicated by the nutritionist is followed, preserving the sense of pleasure as it is made up of the girl's favourite foods. We will then see how this plan will need to be modified depending on the patient's responses, both at the level of her real eating behaviour – that is, what she actually feeds herself – and at the level of the physiological needs found through the medical examinations. Finally, since this girl, unlike the majority of anorexia sufferers, has not yet developed an obsession with weighing her food (another pathogenic behaviour that contributes to maintaining and exacerbating the pathology, and one that is often iatrogenic as a consequence of health interventions), the mother is encouraged to refrain from doing this. When it becomes necessary to measure the quantity of foods eaten during the following sessions, the mother, and only the mother, will be told to use weighing scales, taking care not to show the weight to the daughter. In this way, we avoid structuring a rigid behaviour, limiting the recovery of a healthy balance, as it would hinder or prevent all meals outside the family context due to the impossibility of measuring food quantities in the absence of weighing scales. At the same time, the patient gets used to estimating appropriate portion sizes with her eyes, gradually overcoming the typical fear of the full plate.

Second session

CT: So, P., have you thought about what we said last time?
P: Yes, a lot.
CT: And, listen, did you follow the diet plan, or have you chosen the other road, that of the tube and the drip-feed? — *Investigation on the effects of the first session* —
P: No, I mean, I ate according to the diet plan, especially after the examination I had on Tuesday, because it didn't go very well, and I got even more scared.
T: I'd expected as much. This is the reason I wanted you to do that.
M: In fact, it also came out that they wanted to admit her to hospital, as she's completely dehydrated. She only drinks water and just a little, and she doesn't want anything else. The doctor said that this is serious because she's very dehydrated.
T: What happened after Tuesday?
P: Drinking mainly, they'd like me to drink things like Gatorade, but I don't like that very much.
M: Supplements, minerals.
T: Yes.
P: So maybe I could increase the amount of water. Then in the morning I drink also a juice box and ice tea, but Gatorade ...
T: OK, let's be very clear, P.. Foods contain a percentage of water, and many of them are actually more than 70% water ... You just need to eat more and include certain foods. If you eat healthily, you'll absorb water from your food in addition to what you drink. However, I'd like to know what you did over the past few days. What did she eat? Please tell us [speaking to the mother]. — *Investigation addressed to the mother on the daughter's daily eating regimen: meals, type of foods, quantities* —
M: So ...
T: Did you see if P. increased her food intake, or hasn't it increased?
M: No, the quantities are the same, but she eats — honestly, she eats. Only today she ate a plate of rice and then some meat — though not a lot — then salad, a beer, and some water. She also said she ate a sandwich at school, but I can't be sure of that.
T: OK, and breakfast at home?
M: With us at home she has a glass of fruit juice and two biscuits.
T: Just today, or yesterday and the other days as well?
M: No, yesterday as well, though let's say not immediately. We came on Saturday ... let's say from Tuesday onwards. In particular, she started having the sandwiches from Tuesday onwards.
P: Yes.
M: And since Tuesday, she has started to make an effort, after ...

CT: ... the examination at the centre.

M: That's right, Doctor, after the examination because they wanted to admit her and, in their opinion, it should have been done already ...

T: P., do you think that what your mother has told us is correct, or do you want to add any clarification?

P: It's all correct.

T: What was her weight? – *Weekly investigation on weight* –

M: 40 kilograms, I don't know if you want to see the records ...

T: Yes.

M: They didn't give us the other records. We only have the ECG because we went privately. The other records are at the centre. However, about her weight, my husband was there and asked afterward because he wasn't in the examination room. What did they do to you, P., exactly?

P: They put some patches on my hand and on my right foot.

T: Yes.

P: Then they made me lie down, and then they weighed me and measured my height.

M: And waist measurement maybe.

P: No, no.

T: OK, body mass indexes, hmm, good.

M: So, let's say that she started eating from Tuesday, but not drinking properly – no, she only drinks water. Frankly, we're quite scared, so we've started insisting on other things as well, like: "Let's add pizza in the evening". We also insist, especially my husband, on orange soda and other soft drinks, but she says, "No"; maybe we're overdoing it now that things have got so ...

T: Do you remember what I told you last time, yeah?

M: Yes – definitely. I told my husband about it. I don't know if he also needs to come to the next session.

T: Yes, bring him as well. The more you insist, the more she'll entrench herself. She must be responsible. She knows that if her weight doesn't increase, then she'll end up in hospital with a tube attached to her. This has to be clear – there are no alternatives. – *Restructuring to generate aversion towards the parent's dysfunctional behaviour* –

M: Oh, yes, yes.

T: How did you manage to defer the hospital admission?

M: We said: "No, no. We'll see". My husband was there ... We told the doctor that we'd wait a while, and she replied that the situation isn't that serious, however, she told my husband to come back on Tuesday. So, on Tuesday at 12.30 pm we'll have to go there.

T: Perfect, you'll go back there.

M: Because ... she doesn't want to go back and ...

T: No, [speaking to P.] you'll absolutely go back there ... If we see that you've gained weight then you won't have to go back there again, OK? ... So, to be very clear: you can only avoid being admitted if you keep on course, as your mother told us that you're doing, and we see that your weight starts increasing.
P: But I think if I go there they'll give me drugs.
T: That is always up to you and your parents: deciding whether or not to do it. Nobody can force you, this must be clear.
M: Yes, yes. In fact I actually said: "Let's see what the professor says".
T: So, P., as I said last time, the decision is up to your parents, they're responsible for you, so they'll decide. But we want you to show us that you are keeping on course, OK? If you keep eating like you've eaten today and yesterday then it's inevitable that you'll start recovering your weight ... Unless you use other tricks, hmm. [Speaking to the parents] Does she still use tissues while eating? Does she go to the toilet after meals? – *Investigation addressed to the mother on food elimination or compensating behaviours* –
M: No, No ... I mean, not right after eating. Actually she helps me, to be honest – she helps me wash the dishes. No, this problem with spitting into paper tissues – it's not happening anymore.
T: You haven't done it since, right? And you haven't vomited?
P: No.
M: I don't see her doing this anymore, whereas before it was constant.
T: OK ... this is a major change. Well, I'm glad. How did you stop? Because that takes strength ...
P: I gulp it down.
T: You gulp it down [he smiles]. Gulp it down, you close your eyes and gulp it down – you exert yourself. Well done! That makes me happy and I really appreciate what you're doing because I know how much it costs you. This is very important. – *Positive reinforcement of the patient's functional behaviour* –
M: Yes, it is.
T: Well, then this is a great little achievement.
M: Yes ... well, Doctor, she is doing something in the morning as soon as she gets up, but she said: "Mum, I just can't stop doing it in the morning". But it's only in the morning at the moment.
T: What does she do?
M: She spits.
T: OK, but you haven't eaten anything yet.
M: No, before breakfast, as soon as she gets up ...
T: Well, then I can allow it P., but you mom ... – *we don't intervene with a minor pathological behaviour to avoid encouraging the girl's resistance* –
M: ... But I haven't seen her doing it during the day anymore to be honest.
T: At the moment, it's important that you stay with your daughter at mealtimes ...

M: Yes, yes. We know … But tomorrow, P's asked to stay at school for lunch because she has something going on.
T: To stay at school …
M: Yes, she needs to stay at school.
T: Where do you eat at school? In the cafeteria?
M: No.
P: No, I buy a sandwich or a slice of pizza.
M: This isn't a usual thing – it's because they have tutoring.
P: But we don't know for sure yet.
T: Ok, if it does happen … it's up to you, P. We're just the ones who measure things, OK? I'm happy with the fact that you've been able to stop spitting out what you eat – that's great! But now we need to stay on course, otherwise there's the tube and they'll blow you up like a balloon … So, I'll repeat, it's important that this "bad" examination takes place because they're doing something that's needed, OK? In the sense that they're doing it instead of us, otherwise we'd need to do it because we need those measurements. – *Incentivising functional behaviour and using the redundant analogical image of the nasogastric tube –*
M: The doctor wants to speak with P. on Tuesday, I think …
T: Yes, yes … it's always up to you to decide.
M: Yes, yes – she absolutely didn't want to go, but now we have to …
T: No, No, you, P., you need to listen. I'll repeat: nobody can force you to do anything if your parents don't decide to do it, but I need you to understand that that's the alternative. So, either we do it in a gentle way as we are doing – even though I know it's hard, I know it's very hard – or otherwise, there's the drastic method … And among other things, I can assure you that, unfortunately in many cases, it doesn't solve the problem because often when a girl starts a course of force-feeding, she's on and off, on and off … Essentially, either one recovers one's personal balance or it's a disaster.
M: That's why we rely on you so much, we're putting our trust in you, and I think you also understand the effort on our part, because we're also scared, you know …
T: You must be. However, I repeat: it's important that next time you come with your husband, but you need to avoid forcing her. There are meals, you'll have meals, the important thing is that after meals there's no running to the toilet, no more tissues full of food, OK? [Speaking to P.] Well, if you keep on this route, eating what we've been talking about, there's no need to force yourself further, OK? You can increase what you drink a little bit in between meals, agreed? If you go on like this, things will happen on their own, there's no need to add anything else. And you [speaking to the mother] should avoid insisting: "Drink this, eat this". The responsibility must go back to her, because it's the only way to mobilise her

resources, as she's already demonstrated to us. — *Direct prescriptions to the parents and to the patient aimed at incentivising functional behaviours, interrupting dysfunctional behaviours, and making the patient feel responsible —*

M: Yes, yes — that's true, since Tuesday.
T: OK, good. I want to see you on Wednesday, after you've been to the hospital appointment.
M: OK.
T: So, we're staying on course, OK?
M: Yes, we're totally relying on you, here.
T: You must observe without intervening, but you must be there during meals and keep your daughter with you after meals, agreed? [Speaking to P.] So, we'll measure whether, from now until next Tuesday, your weight increases a bit, as we'd like. If you gain just a little bit of weight, then we can avoid all the rest, agreed?
P: Yes.
T: Good ... Let's see you on Wednesday, then.

In the time between the first and the second session the patient has begun to eat a greater amount of food. Her fears of hospitalisation and forced-feeding, outside of her direct control, were also elicited by the medical examination which she had to undergo. These fears have triggered a mobilisation of her resources in the direction of collaboration and therapeutic change. The investigation of the daily eating regimen, which opens the session, is done by listening first to the mother's point of view, and then to the daughter's. By observing this sequence, we obtain a rigorous assessment that, in addition to reaffirming the hierarchical family positions, avoids the patient generating arguments, symmetric attitudes, and closures. In fact, if the young anorexic patients are asked about their adherence to nutrition plans first, they often report eating greater quantities than in reality because, according to their perception, everything that is being swallowed is always too much, and this induces parents to amend their answers. Thus, this turns the session into a kind of duel that endangers the construction of an effective therapeutic relationship, which is so important in the early stages of treatment. Lastly, it should be noted that during the session, thanks to the focused use of non-verbal communication, the therapist oscillates between two positions toward the patient: an assertive and directive position aimed at stopping the most important dysfunctional modes that contribute to the persistence of the pathology, and a more soft and friendly position that is displayed in the presence of functional behaviours. It is precisely this relational shade that determines the authority of the therapist, allowing him or her to become a reference point for the young patient.

Third session

T: So, P., since our last session, did you do anything that we agreed upon? – *Investigating the change process* –
P: I kept following the diet plan.
T: Which one, yours or the doctor's?
P: The doctor's.
T: And has the weight that's written here changed compared to the previous measurement? – *Weekly weight evaluation* –
P: They didn't weigh me yesterday.
T: So, is this the weight from the last time?
M: Yes, ten days ago. They wanted to do it this way ... I'd like her to have gained a kilogram. They rebuked me and told me that it'd be worse if she had gained a kilogram: it's like if someone goes 300 miles per hour and then suddenly brakes, she'd go off the road and slam into a wall.
T: That's an interesting theory. So ...
M: I don't know if she has gained weight. At home there's a weighing scale. If she wants, she can weigh herself. I didn't weigh her; she's a grown-up, she can weigh herself if she wants.
T: No, she's not grown up, Madam ...[4] – *Redefinition aimed at responsibilising parents* –
M: No, she's not grown up, so we have to force her. Please tell us what to do.
T: Otherwise there's the hospital ... P., I am willing to help you, but the rules must be respected. If we want to avoid hospitalisation, I have to see your weight increasing week by week. If your weight doesn't go up, then the tube becomes necessary ... So, once you get out of here, I want you to go home, weigh yourself, and call me. And I want a weight measurement once a week, every week, because it's clear that if the trend is an increase in weight – let's forget about the theory of braking at 300 miles per hour – it's very good if you do it gradually.
M: I had a shock when I read those values. I hope that then slowly ...
T: I'm sorry, but please read them again, OK? In one sense, the interpretation is very negative, but if you read the rest of the data, it's not like that. We have margins to work to, but these margins can shrink quickly. We're still at about 40 kilograms, and the danger zone is under 36 kilograms. Her dehydration is not so severe, the body mass index indicates she's underweight, but her life is not imminently at risk. What it's important to understand now is whether she is going in a certain direction or if she's not going in that direction. So we need to have a weekly check ... Do you agree, P.? So, later, you go home, you weigh yourself without clothes, and you call me.

When you said you followed the diet plan, tell me, what did you eat exactly from your point of view? And then we'll listen to your parents. — *Evaluation of the quantity and type of food eaten* —

P: In the morning, a small bottle of fruit juice and two biscuits. At 11.00 am, a sandwich or a slice of pizza plus ice tea, lately. At lunch, I have first and second courses with reduced portions and, above all, I've been drinking.

T: I want to understand, by how much are the portions reduced, exactly? How much pasta do you eat for lunch?

P: Around 50 grams.

M: Less.

T: So you eat a third of a regular portion.

M: It's small, yes; she leaves the sauce, she avoids everything.

T: It's natural that she does that, otherwise she'd have solved the problem. Does she eat meat?

M: A small slice.

T: Bread?

M: Very little, 10, maybe 15 grams ...

T: And any side dish?

M: Salad, and she drinks a sip of water.

P: I'm drinking water.

M: OK, let's say a glass.

T: Then ...

P: In the afternoon, a yogurt or a fruit juice box with something ... In the evening, it depends, a slice of pizza or soup with some cheese.

T: OK, let me ask you a question. After all, this is what's worrying you: how many calories do you think you're eating in a day? — *De-structuring erroneous beliefs on daily caloric intake with the use of analogical and explanatory language* —

P: I don't know.

M: I have no idea.

T: You're sure you don't know.

P: Honestly, I don't know.

T: OK, when the dietician gave you the diet plan ...

M: It was more or less written so that if you follow it entirely it's about 1,700 calories.

T: OK, and you, eating like this, how many do you think you're getting?

P: A bit less because the quantities are smaller, so maybe 1,300? I don't know.

T: OK, you see what happens to all the girls who have a problem like yours: your perception of the size of things is altered. You're like Alice in Wonderland who sees everything big, OK? You're eating less than half of what was recommended; you're on 700 calories a day and it's clear that you can't get better this way. To reassure you: in the morning, for breakfast, you're having around 80 calories. When you have your mid-morning snack, though you've only recently started having it, it's about 200 calories and you're up to 280. What you eat for lunch is 30 grams of pasta, 109 calories, and we are at 389. The meat you eat, 30 grams, is 30 calories, 419 ... The bread, 27 calories and we are at 446, then with vegetables we arrive at 461 ... What you have in the afternoon doesn't reach 100 calories, let's say 70 ... 531. In the evening, it's more or less the same as what you get for lunch, so 184 calories. You're barely reaching 715 calories, so tube feeding is inevitable, is that clear? Now I'll ask you a direct question: is it harder for you to increase what you eat by adding different foods or would it be easier to increase what you eat by eating more single things 'instead of putting lots of different foods together?[5] For example, at lunchtime, is it easier for you to eat a plate of pasta, but a good-sized plate of pasta, or is it easier to eat different things, like you are doing now: pasta, meat, and bread? – *Strategically oriented question aimed at finding the most suitable therapeutic meal plan for the patient –*

P: Perhaps a bigger plate of pasta, maybe.

T: [Speaking to the mother] And then some fruit because we need liquids, OK? But she doesn't have to know about it.

M: But with fruit ... she only eats half an apple or half a pear.

T: But if we eliminate meat and bread and increase the pasta, then she has to eat a good amount of fruit: strawberries, kiwi ... OK? – *Recalling observance and adherence to the therapeutic indications –*

M: Bananas?

T: Those in the morning. [Speaking to P.] I'm trying to give you an indication, let's see if you respect it, OK? I'll repeat: if you follow me, we can come out of this without hospital and without torture. If you don't follow me, it will be inevitable, all right? In the morning, add a banana to what you already eat, that's 88 calories, but we need it for its components, especially potassium. Can you do that? Look, I'm planning everything with you. Your parents won't nag you to "eat, eat"; they'll just prepare the food for you, OK? Perfect, then mid-morning a sandwich/slice of pizza; at lunch, instead of making things difficult – because in these cases, one tends to "bury" everything, and the more things there are, the more soil we have – it must be 100 grams of pasta, but without any meat sauce or she'll get scared, OK? ... Tomato sauce, but don't worry if she doesn't eat the sauce ... Then you prepare a mixture of kiwi and strawberries. Do you like those? – *Negotiating foods with the patient –*

P: Yes, yes.

T: But a good-sized amount. In the afternoon, it's up to you – have whatever you fancy. Then in the evening, you'll only have to eat either 150 grams of lean meat with vegetables and a little bit of bread, 30 grams, or 200 grams of fish.

M: She doesn't like fish.

T: Cheese is OK as well, 150 grams, I guess she eats only low-fat cheese ...

F AND M TOGETHER: Yes.
T: But make sure you change foods with each meal, because we must preserve taste and avoid following mechanical nutrition, otherwise it becomes torturous. Do you accept this, P?
P: Yes, but, for example, do I have to eat meat every night?
T: Meat, cheese, or pizza, you can choose. I'm giving you a plan close to 900 calories now.
Last question: what physical activity are you doing now? – *Evaluating the presence of exercising* –
P: Nothing.
T: Because the report says compulsive swimming.
M: At school, twice a week.
T: That's good for you. Do you walk a lot?
F: Stairs, willingly and often.
T: OK ... you need to keep an eye on that, because we must evaluate everything. Please, call and tell us her weight. – *Prescription to parents: observing food intake and the presence of excessive motor activity, without direct intervention* –
M: Does she have to go back to the hospital on Tuesday?
T: Yes, yes.
P: I don't want to go there.
T: OK, but you have to earn that. We have to be drastic about this, all right?
P: Do I necessarily have to go?
T: If you can show me that your weight has gone up, then we can avoid it. See you next week!

Fourth session

T: Welcome. What's the situation? Who wants to start? – *Investigating the change process* –
M: I'll start, as always ... In short, she had to gain weight, do you remember, Professor? But instead when we weighed her – I'd bought a digital scale – the dial just sat there, on 40 kilograms ... 40.1, 40.15 ... But she'd followed the diet plan quite well.
T: Better to say the indications provided ...
M: OK, yes, the indications that you gave us.
T: Let's eliminate the word "diet".
M: She followed them OK, in the sense that we aren't sure if she eats the sandwich in the morning or her afternoon snack. For example, probably on Saturday and Sunday, she definitely skipped . And the fruit is a little more limited, in the sense that instead of a good-sized plate, as you said, she eats one kiwi, some strawberries, or maybe a pear or an apple; however, even when she does eat the strawberries, it's not a whole plate ...

T: I have to say, I'd anticipated something like this ... let's say it was expected. Everything that isn't under control is seen as bad and is reduced, [speaking to P.] right?
P: Yes.
M: And this is despite the fact that she had lunch and dinner with us, as you said.
T: So, did she follow the rules we gave her?
M: Yes, yes, I'd have to say yes ... [speaking to her husband] right? In general, yes. For example, she eats 100 grams of pasta at lunch, and in the evening she has 150 grams of meat or cheese or pizza.
T: And the same in the morning?
M: Yes ... in the morning she has a banana. She's skipped it maybe one morning.
T: Good.
M: Yes ... breakfast. Yes, but she's a little bit worried because there hasn't been any weight gain ...
T: Well, OK, let's talk about this ... What we agreed upon last time was certainly not enough to indicate that she'd gain weight: if we exclude the mid-morning sandwich, but even if we include it, doing quick calculations we don't reach 1,000 calories, and in this way it's impossible to gain weight. To do that, we must go further. But in these cases, we can't suddenly start making her eat too much, because she will get scared.
M: Yes, then she says she doesn't like the idea.
T: Of course, it's obvious ... I'm happy because, for me, the first goal was to establish a relationship that allowed you, P., to start getting varied nutrition, eating things that usually girls like you don't even want to look at – like pasta and bananas – things that are usually considered off limits. Bananas are considered overly sugary things and pasta a high-calorie thing that makes your stomach and thighs swell. For me, this is already a big step, but it's clear that it's not enough. It's the first step, the first step to which we must add other steps. But slowly, because what we're doing here is carving a diamond: if we hit it too strongly, we'll break it, but if we hit it too gently, we won't engrave the right area ... – *Positive reinforcement to the patient on the results achieved with redefinition of the therapeutic objectives through the use of analogic language* –
M: Yes, yes.
T: Were you scared of what you ate or was it OK for you? – *Discerning strategic question* –
P: Well, maybe at the beginning the pasta seemed like a lot.
T: At the beginning ...
P: And also dinner, both.
T: Then ...
P: Then, now it's a bit better.

T: OK, very good. So, you can see that you're getting used to it. We get used to everything, you know? Just like how over time you got used to reducing, reducing, reducing to the point where only a small amount seemed like such a lot to you, it also works in reverse: you get used to it gradually.
P: Yes.
T: Have you been nervous, agitated or have you been calmer?[6] – *Discerning strategic question* –
P: At times, when I sat down to eat, I was calmer.
T: Good ... and how's your life outside your relationship with food?[7] – *Strategically oriented question* –
P: Yes.
T: "Yes" ... What does that mean? What happens at school and in your social life?
P: Well, there's always a little thought about this problem.
T: What is the thought?
P: Well, maybe that ... because, when I weigh myself, I can see that I'm not gaining weight.
T: OK ... so the thought in this case is, "why isn't my weight going up?"
P: No, well, I mean ... now that I'm eating more, I'm feeling even better.
T: Ah ...
P: So, I also thought that my weight was going up because I'm feeling better.
T: [Smiling] Nice connection.
CT: "I eat, I gain weight".
T: No, "I eat, I feel better, I gain weight".
CT: In a week.
T: If only it were like that.
CT: If only.
P: But then, I went and weighed myself and there was no change.
M: There was also a moment of panic at home because one of the mornings she weighed herself ...
T: She'd lost weight.
M: And then she told me that she'd lost weight ... She'd gone down to 39 and she got scared. I got angry and I told her: now you're going to hospital, even if nobody else says so.
T: Well done!
M: There, she got scared; she said, "No ... No ..." But she was well, she had actually lost weight.
T: The type of nutrition we introduced, although it exceeds the one that she was following before in terms of calories, has a superior component of proteins that are mostly consumed in the evening, unlike the carbohydrate-rich dishes that P. was eating before. So, in addition to activating her metabolism and helping her to gain lean body mass, the glycemic load and insulin are kept low; those are often responsible for inflammatory

phenomena, swelling, and, if taken to the extreme, getting fat. — *Restructuring the introduced therapeutic nutrition plan through explanatory language* —
M: Yes, yes.
T: But then P. has recovered her weight and recovered it in a different way. It's essential at her age to gain lean body mass, composed of muscles that feed on protein.
M: Yes, in fact, now I've weighed her for three mornings, though perhaps, I don't know if that's wrong ... you told us once a week ... but since I was so worried ... every morning before breakfast I weigh her, naked.
T: All right, and the hospital is still there.
F: It's also nearby.
M: Yes, that's true ...
T: It would only take a moment, there's the E.R. department, then quickly a feeding tube, a drip, it's all very fast. [Speaking to the father] So, Dad, a bit reassured or still worried?
F: No ... I'm reassured, partly because I can see that she's applying herself — that should definitely be acknowledged — but on the other hand, I can also see that she is having to make a terrible effort.
T: It is like this at the beginning.
F: And the fact that maybe I'm the first to make a mistake, in the sense that I say: "Try ..."
T: No, avoid doing that, you must absolutely avoid doing that ... — *Calling parents to observe and adhere to the prescriptions: 1. observing without direct intervention, 2. Waiting one hour with the daughter after meals* —
F: But I watch her: if she eats a banana, she picks it apart, she picks it apart entirely, she takes the filaments off, she chisels all of it ...
T: But this is their style, the style of girls like her ...
F: Two biscuits ...
M: Also, such a small amount of bread ...
T: But, forgive me, every time you intervene, you're not helping me to help her. She knows what her doses are. Today we'll increase them a little bit and she must get by ... You just have to stay there, unresponsive, until she's finished. That's it. But you must avoid saying, "Come on, come on, eat it" — you really must avoid this. You just have to stay there and also, as we discussed, stay with her for an hour after meals, OK?
M: One hour. P. doesn't stay there that long.
T: One hour. This is your job, OK?
F: We haven't been doing this.
T: But you must do it.
M: Maybe we misunderstood, then ...
F: Because she leaves immediately ...
M: No, not immediately, she stays for little while, but I haven't thought about an hour, here, frankly.
T: Mmh, mmh.

M: Yes, and she must stay there with us.
T: An hour is the minimum ... just because I want to avoid any other kind of risk, OK?
M: Understood, P.?!
F: Come and study with me and we'll work on your homework.
T: Yes, yes, he's right, P. [Speaking to the mother] He can go with her without any problems. You know, P., I'm putting so much trust in you, but since I'm not working just on you, I'm also working on a pathology that's become, as you well know, like another person living inside you. It's like this other guest that we must hold off, because it might be tempted to do other things, to not follow us. So, it's not like I'm discrediting you, I'm discrediting that other part of you, the one we have to absolutely keep at bay, OK?[8] – *Using ambivalent communication with the patient to reinforce the therapeutic relationship and lower the resistance to change (therapeutic double bind)* –
M: But then sometimes, excuse me Professor, always in relation to this topic ... For example, she'll have dinner with her friends tonight – it happens at least once a week.
T: But thank goodness it happens, it's important to have this. – *Positive redefinition and reinforcement of the patient's social-relational activities with her peers* –
M: So it's clear that on these nights we can't monitor her.
T: But going out with friends is important. However, she has learned that she'll be monitored in the morning by being weighed on the scale, right?
M: Of course, of course we do that. There's weighing her on the scale.
T: There's the scale and there's the E.R. nearby, we know that. Where are you going tonight, P.? What are you going to eat, pizza?
P: Yes.
T: So, it's OK.
M: It's her birthday, by the way.
T: How old will you be tonight?
P: Fifteen.
T: Ah, well, I'm very happy. So you know, right, we have to increase the dosage a little bit? [The patient smiles] I saw a smile that has become a grimace, right? But we must do this ... we have to increase it a little bit, OK? ... And we must increase it a little bit in each of the three main meals. It's clear that it would be good if you always ate the sandwich mid-morning, but since we're talking to that other part of you, I don't know if that part will make you eat it or not, so instead we have to increase the amount where we can control the other part. I'd like the two morning biscuits to become three, along with the banana. All right? It's not that much, right? Then the pasta, more than 100 grams is no good, because that'd become boring for anyone, right? So we need to add something else ... a little bit of a second course, OK? Just a little bit, OK? And I know that this is an important step, because you have this idea in your mind: "Now I'll eat different foods in the same meal ..." but this is

important, OK? [Speaking to the parents] So, as she wants meat or fish, no more than 50 grams ... Just a little, OK? Dinner will stay the same, but we'll add a little bit of bread, only 50 grams. — *Use of the therapeutic double bind to encourage compliance and adherence to new food indications that include the increase of food intake and the association of different foods —*

M: Last week, she was eating less than 30 grams of bread. In our opinion, that wasn't enough.

T: How much?

M: A little piece. P. prefers flatbread.

T: Well, after all, you prepare the portions. Just don't go overboard with it. 40 grams, OK?

M: Bread or flatbread, OK. At lunch or dinner?

T: In the meal where she doesn't have pasta. So dinner, we said.

P: About 50 grams at dinner, Mum, as he says [pointing to the therapist].

T: Your parents will weigh your food, you'll only see it on the plate at the table, P. I want to reassure you again ... In your opinion, how much did we just add? You're better than me at calculating calories by now, you're a little scientist ... how much did we add? A biscuit, how much is an extra biscuit? 23 extra calories? Am I right?

P: Yes.

T: Look, let's round it up ... 25, OK? 50 grams of extra meat at lunch, lean meat, because you'll eat that, that's 55 calories, OK ... so 80 calories in total. If you were eating — at least for a few days because your parents said that then you reduced it — up to 30 grams of bread, and we add 10 grams, that's another 110 calories. So, actually, we've only added 190 calories. Now I think that, I should tell you, the scale could still throw a tantrum, but we have to accept that. We have to go slowly to get there, OK? — *Incentive for therapeutic compliance through reassurance on the caloric intake introduced —*

P: Yes.

T: Good.

M: Still plenty of fruit?

T: Always, as much as she wants, as well as yogurt, OK? So, P., I'm taking on this important responsibility to help you without resorting to the hospital, and I do it very gladly. However, as you've seen, I'm very stubborn — I want things to be done in a certain way. So far you've done that, and I'm very happy: let's go on this way. [Speaking to the parents] I also told you that between now and next week it might be difficult for you to see her weight go up as much as you'd like. What's important is that we keep the route going slowly, OK? — *Positive reinforcement to the patient and mentioning the possibility of a minimum weight gain to the parents in order to avoid the activation of attempted dysfunctional solutions —*

M: Yes.

T: See you next week!

Fifth session

T: How're you getting on? — *Investigating the change process* —
P: Nothing. This morning I weighed myself like every morning and my weight was 40.6 kilograms.
T: So what does this mean?
P: That I've gained a little bit of weight.
T: But you have gained some. Well, and has this been gradual or just today?
P: No, it's been gradual.
T: It's been gradual.
M: Yes.
T: That is, every day you've seen something.
M: No, well, not exactly. One day it was more. For example 40.7, another morning 40.5 and this morning 40.6. However, there is this weight gain.
T: Good ... So, how much weight have you gained, in your evaluation?
P: Half a kilogram.
T: Perfect.
T: Are you scared about this, or are you happy? — *Discerning strategic question* —
P: No, well, I thought I'd have gained even more because I was eating ...
T: Do you remember that the other time I reassured you about this I told you that, based on what you'd eat, any weight gain would be minimal or non-existent? The "other you" makes you see and believe that your portions are huge, but we've shown that part of you that the opposite is actually true — *Use of the therapeutic double bind to redefine and encourage progress* —
P: Yes.
T: This means that you've been good at respecting what we agreed on.
P: Yes.
T: Without a fuss?
P: More or less.
T: You made a bit of fuss.
P: Yes.
M: No ... She's been good, really. She followed the indications at home. It's only after meals she feels really ... She says, "I can't do it". So, I stay there an hour with her, even if she isn't really having it, but then it's her who tells me: "Mum, come upstairs". It's her who wants this. She just complains a lot that she feels full.
T: But you have to be prepared for this, P.: with the progressive eating restriction, you've slowed down your digestive processes and you've got your stomach used to being half-empty. Now your system has to be trained: by gradually increasing the amount that you eat, that physiological discomfort will disappear, but above all, the psychological discomfort will go away as well, that fear of suddenly becoming a doughnut, and that's the most important bit. Good. [Speaking to the parents] Parents, are you a little more reassured?
F: Yes ... yes, we are a bit more reassured though she still ...

T: ...I did say a little, a little ...
F: ...Yes, yes.
M: Yes, I'm happy because I can see that she ...
T: Is determined, isn't she?
M: Yes, yes, she is eating, a little bit less than ... Amongst other things, she's still not eating less fruit, because she'll eat a pear, an apple, a kiwi, some strawberries but not a good-sized plate as you told us. But, she does always have a banana, every single morning, she's being very good. Today there was ... it wasn't exactly clear, maybe I or she ... because there was cold rice for lunch, a good-sized plate, and since we're having pizza tonight, she had this cold rice and some meat, 50 grams, and she said she didn't have to eat bread or flatbread – in fact, she didn't eat her 40 grams – while I think she did have to eat them.
T: She was right, P. is very precise. We said that the two meals must always be organised with a percentage of carbohydrates and a percentage of protein, OK? In the evening, there's a prevalence of protein, and at lunch there's a prevalence of carbohydrates, but she already had her beautiful plate of rice.
M: So, if this happens ...
T: OK, you can always alternate between the two, as long as in the two meals there's a meal with a prevalence of carbohydrates (i.e., you eat pasta or rice) and then 50 grams of meat, a side dish and fruit; whereas in the evening, you were right, P. In the evening you have your portion of meat, cheese, or fish and 40 grams of bread.
M: So basically today it's a bit messed up because there's pizza.
T: Today it went well. Be aware that pizza contains carbohydrates for the most part but it also has mozzarella, which has a protein component. But above all, it's one of the dishes that your daughter eats with more enjoyment.
M: Yes, yes.
T: This past week, P., beyond a little discomfort, has the idea of eating these foods really cost you a lot of effort or can we keep them, in your opinion? – *Strategic discerning question* –
P: Keep them, yes, but increase them, I don't know.
T: Look, we only have this measure, OK? This has to be clear: if, by eating like this your weight continues to go up, then we're not in any hurry, OK? However, as I said, you've been very precise, to the second. We want half a kilogram a week, and if we keep going on like that, it's perfect, just a high-precision Swiss watch; but if we find that your weight isn't going up, then next time we'll need to make adjustments and increase something, OK? – *Using the "go slow" technique to avoid encouraging resistance to change* –
P: Yes.

T: Now the most important thing about what we're doing is that, given that P. knows her likes and dislikes, we need to make sure that these are followed and stimulated. So, if tonight there's pizza that you like so much ...

P: Yes.

T: ... Perfect, that's fine. And there can't be any rigidity in the daily and weekly intake. The important thing is that now we begin to introduce the concept of pleasure, which is the real antagonist of your problem. – *Restructuring the importance of flexibility and pleasure in the patient's nutrition plan* –

When someone develops a problem like yours, you know what the first feeling is, right? What you once liked first becomes menacing, then frightening, then it causes disgust, and then you don't want to see it anymore, until it provokes a phobia, right? We're walking the opposite path, OK? And nobody wants you to get fat, only to be as beautiful and as fit as you can be. At that point, at best, we'll stabilise the result ... And we should get you to eat what you like most while paying attention to your weight. We can get there without any problems, you just need to follow a certain type of training. The way you're doing now, you're all doing well. What kind of life are you having now? The usual, or are you a bit isolated? – *Discerning strategic question* –

P: No, compared to what I was doing before, when I was playing volleyball, I don't do anything anymore.

T: So you go to school in the morning but, after school, do you stay at home in the afternoon or do you go out and meet people?

P: Usually when there isn't much homework I go out.

T: So, you have your friends.

P: Yes, yes.

T: OK, fine. Then we just have to keep on course. So, if we find that this week your weight continues to go up, there's no problem. If your weight is the same then, the next time we meet, we'll need to re-arrange your eating plan together, OK? That's it. The direction is good. – *Positive reinforcement to the patient and to the parents and a reference to the maintenance of the therapeutic route* –

M: Yes, but she keeps complaining; she's afraid she won't make it.

T: It's all right. You know that we want half a kilogram a week, no more, no less. Just be a Swiss watch like you were this time, OK?

P: Yes.

F: Excuse me, Professor, could supplements be useful?

T: If we give her supplements, they'd replace the foods that she needs to go back to appreciating for the pleasure of eating them. At the moment, this is what helps us the most.

F AND M: OK.

T: See you next week. Goodbye.

After four sessions since the beginning of the therapy, the first weight gain of half a kilogram was obtained with the introduction of a nutrition plan that includes the association of carbohydrates and protein in each meal, and the increase of portion sizes. To unblock the rigid perceptive-reactive anorexic system against food and to avoid relapses, it is important that the patient gradually accepts eating meals which combine different types of foods. Moreover, it is essential that she progressively chooses her favourite foods with more freedom, following her tastes. Precisely for this reason, parents are reassured about transgressions to the established plan that the daughter has spontaneously allowed herself. In fact, these behaviours indicate a greater flexibility in the perceptions, cognitions and behaviours in relation to nutrition, which are accompanied by the important presence of pleasure, not only with respect to food but also with respect to relational and social life. This is, therefore, positively reinforced. In this way, we continue to encourage parental behaviours and attitudes which are functional to the remission of the pathology, and we stop dysfunctional behaviours. For example, at this stage of the therapeutic process, the inclusion of food supplements, which are often given to patients with anorexia, frequently becomes an attempted solution that contributes to the maintenance of the problem; in fact, supplements demotivate patients even more in relation to eating as they believe they have already taken what is enough to guarantee their survival and health. In the following months the girl continued to gain half a kilogram per week until she completely recovered her target weight, with a healthy nutrition plan, but based on flexibility and pleasure. She also resumed her physical activity and social life, including her first adolescent romance. Today, the young, formerly anorexic girl is 23 years old and studies psychology.

Case 2

This case differs markedly from Case 1 due to the "apparent ease" with which the patient's full therapeutic collaboration was obtained. This case was selected as a good example of very brief therapy for juvenile anorexic disorder. The following are the complete transcripts of the entire therapeutic process, which consisted of ten sessions, including the first follow-up after three months. This does not mean that this case was easy to treat. On the contrary, it required considerable work on the personal and interpersonal aspects related to the pathology.

First session

T: Therapist; CT: Co-therapist P: Patient; M: Mother; F: Father

- T: Good evening, what problem brings you here? [The mother points at the daughter]
- T: Can you describe it in the most concrete way possible? – *Operational definition of the problem* –

M: In 2009 she started a diet because she weighed 63 kilograms. She wanted to lose weight because she'd always been a few kilograms overweight; she wanted to be beautiful. But then she started controlling her food intake a little too much and losing weight too fast. When her period stopped, we started to get worried because she was doing physical activity – volleyball – and she was no longer able to keep up with sports. We turned to the general hospital where they provide group therapy.
T: Group or family therapy?
M: Parental therapy and group therapy for girls. But even with the help of a nutritionist we could see that she wasn't improving. Actually, she was absorbing all the negative information and behaviours from the group and it was making the situation worse. We've reached a point where she's now trembling in front of food, she's afraid of eating, everything seems always too much, she has sudden panic attacks, she's jumpy, she's terrified, and she sees herself as fat. Her legs look very big to her, so she's always afraid of eating. Now she eats mainly vegetables. Even if we put bread on the table, she barely touches it. In terms of carbohydrates at breakfast, she'll barely eat one biscuit. She hasn't had her period in two years. Now she's also left school because she says she can't concentrate. She's in her fourth year at a linguistic high school. She's always had excellent grades, but unfortunately now ...
T: Does she still have a social life or has she withdrawn from it? – *Strategically oriented question* –
M: Let's just say that she used to see people, but now she only has two or three friends that she meets up with frequently. Now that she's left school, she doesn't even want to stay at home in the morning, she comes with me at my workplace. I work as a janitor at a school. No, she doesn't have many friends.
T: OK, OK. [Speaking to the patient] Were you forced to come here or did you want to come? – *Discerning strategic question* –
P: No ... Actually, my mum told me about this centre and ... no, I wanted to come.
T: So, do you think you have a problem that needs to be solved or do you think you don't have it? – *Discerning strategic question* –
P: There is a problem ...
T: Can you describe it? What's your problem? [Brief pause]
P: I'm no longer able to eat – I don't know how to eat and I can no longer see myself as I really am.
T: OK, fine. So, do you recognise that you're wearing magnifying lenses when you look at yourself, or don't you think so? – *Discerning strategic question* –
P: Sometimes I can see myself as I really am.
T: And do you see yourself as fat right now, as extremely fat, or not? – *Discerning strategic question* –

P: Most of the time, yes.
T: And when you say: "I don't know how to eat", do you mean that everything seems too much for you? – *Strategically oriented question* –
P: Yes.
T: OK, good. But you've also told me, "I'm aware that this is a problem". So the next question is: do you want to solve this problem, or do you think it's impossible to solve? – *Discerning strategic question* –
P: I want to solve it.
T: Good, so if I ask you to do things in conflict with your feelings, will you try to do them? – *Discerning strategic question* –
P: I'll do them.
T: Well, this is already a step forward. I'm really glad. What do you eat during the day? – *Investigation on daily nutrition: types and quantities of food consumed* –
P: For breakfast, most of the time a cappuccino or a cup of tea with biscuits … almost nothing …
T: What does "almost nothing" mean? A biscuit?
P: Sometimes a biscuit or half a piece of toast.
T: That gets you through to lunch?
P: Yes.
T: What do you have for lunch?
P: Pasta … any kind of soup … but only a very small amount.
T: How much pasta do you eat?
P: Less than 50 grams.
T: OK.
P: And after lunch I have some fruit.
T: Good.
P: And fruit as a snack.
T: Then you get to dinner and what do you have?
P: What everyone else eats, but a small amount … a really small amount. In fact, when I go to bed I feel dizzy.
T: I would guess you do.
P: Some fruit …
T: OK, listen. What do you do during the day? What's your typical day?[9] – *Strategically oriented question* –
P: At the moment, I go to the elementary school with my mum until 2 pm. Otherwise, like if we don't go out, I stay at home and I occasionally go out with friends.
T: OK, so you go to work with your mum, and otherwise you stay at home …
P: Mmh, yes.
T: Is the family all here or do you have any siblings? – *Survey on the family system* –
M: She has a younger brother – he's 13 years old.

T: Good. What role does dad play in this situation? – *Investigation of attempted paternal solutions* –
F: I try to do everything that I possibly can. As I'm ignorant on the subject, sometimes I keep quiet because I don't know whether or not I'll be helping ...
T: Sure ...
F: Most of the time we go out with her. Mostly we'll go shopping, or get a coffee. She's always happy to go out; she doesn't like staying at home.
T: With you, of course ... Going out with you, though ...
F: She's very clever ... she wants to go bowling, play pool, so ...
T: You do dad things! [All laugh]
P: I like going bowling.
T: Well, it's fun. Good.
F: She was playing volleyball and going swimming. She was really athletic – that is, she was playing in the upper categories because she was so good. She liked sports ... She still likes them, but she doesn't have the strength to do them any longer ... She likes clothes, likes to look pretty and I think that's a good thing ...
T: Sort of ...
F: Everyone can learn to be beautiful if they want to ... why isn't that a good thing?
T: Let's say that it's half good and half bad ...
M: It's the beginning of the problem. [They nod]
M: Professor ... if it helps, we're separated. So we see each other mainly in the evening when the family is reunited. We have dinner together, but then the rest of the day everyone's on their own. The children stay with me, and then we meet up in the evening.
T: Do you have another family?
F: No, no ... we're legally separated, but we're still "together", as it were. We don't see each other in the morning because I go to work, she goes to work, and we get together at 6:30–7:00 pm after work.
T: But you do sleep under the same roof?
F: Not at the moment, because my mother isn't well so I'm still sleeping at her place, even though she has a care provider, but I have to go back to sleeping in the same house as my daughter as soon as I can. [He strokes her hair]
T: Can I ask you how long you've been separated? – *Strategically oriented questions* –
M: Three years, almost four.
T: How long ago did the disorder appear?[10]
M: Her decision to start the diet was made after the separation.
P: After ... I started the diet in November.
M: A few months after we left home.
T: What's the reason you left the house?

M: Oh, well ... he stayed at the house and we left.
T: OK, so mother and children moved to another house.
M: Yes.
T: [Speaking to the patient] So, are you willing to follow my advice even if I'm going to tell you what to eat? Let's do a therapeutic experiment, OK? Let's measure what you're able to do, OK? – *Setting up an agreement with the patient* –
P: Mmh, yes.
T: Well then, what I'd like from you is that we gradually get up to proper nutrition, which for a girl like you means no less than 1,400 calories and no more than 1,600 calories per day. Here's my premise: nobody wants to make you get fat, we only want you to be as beautiful and as fit as possible. So I'll never want to make you fat, OK? In fact I told you: no more than 1,600 calories but not less than 1,400. I'm also telling you this because there's one thing that you don't know and that most of your peers don't know. Sometimes you can eat very little and strangely not lose weight, or even gain weight because your metabolism slows down. And often, you could tend to swell due to eating restriction and inflammatory processes. This happens when your calorie intake is below a certain level. Is that clear? But, if you let me help you, we can put everything back in the right place, OK? But I want to ask you a question first: how much should you weigh, in your opinion?
P: 50.
T: Perfect, we agree.
P: Because before, I was ...
T: You were too ...
P: At 50 I had finished the diet.
T: 50 kilograms, that's perfect for you. I agree. So there are no tricks, OK? – *Agreement on the weight to be achieved* –
P: Yes.
T: Well, if there was no chance you could get fat, which biscuits would you most like to eat in the morning? Your favourite? – *Evoking pleasure of food* –
P: I like lemon biscuits.
T: Can you buy those, or does your mum make them?
P: No, we buy them.
T: What are they? I'm not familiar with them.
M: They're dry biscuits, lemon-flavored shortbread biscuits!
T: You and I must agree on everything – calculate the calories of what you eat together – to get you to eat the right way, but based on the things you like because what helps us tackle your problem is for you to indulge in and take pleasure from food, but in a controlled way. So, you're afraid that if you let yourself take pleasure in eating, you'll go back to being 63 kilograms, right? – *Negotiation of the daily nutrition regimen with the patient* –

P: Yes. Sometimes ... sometimes, um ... sometimes some small biscuits ...
T: You indulge in them, don't you?
P: No, but I'd like to. But then I'd also like a piece of cake, Professor!
T: So, in the morning, these famous biscuits. In your opinion, how many calories do they contain?
P: Maybe 50 ...
T: 44 calories per biscuit. If you eat five of them, it's 220 calories. If you drink a cappuccino it's 300 calories. Can we allow ourselves that?
P: Mmh, it can be done.
T: Good, we allow ourselves that, right? [She nods]
T: In the morning, 300 calories. Do you usually have pasta for lunch?
M: I alternate pasta with vegetables or beans.
T: Do you like pasta?
P: Pasta for lunch ... yeah, I like it.
T: That's good, good. How many calories are there in 100 grams of pasta, in your opinion?
P: 300
T: 365 calories to be precise, plus sauce, that's 400–420 calories. Can we allow that?
P: At the moment I'm eating less than that ...
T: I know, but I'm telling you that we have to reach a certain number of calories because otherwise your body defends itself: it slows its metabolism down and accumulates fat mass and toxins. We don't want cellulite, right? It's horrible, isn't it?! [She nods]
T: OK, so 100 grams, that's 330 calories, plus seasoning and we're at around 400 calories. We can allow that, right?
P: Mmh.
T: Also, if we add the 300 calories you'll eat in the morning, then we'll reach 700 calories and we are well under the target, OK? Do you like to eat fruit after pasta?
P: Yes.
T: Which fruit do you like best?
P: Oranges.
T: Very well. That's 74 calories, a nice big orange, OK? We are now at 774 calories. We're still well under ... Do you go straight to dinner or do you have a snack?
P: I always eat fruit, an apple or a banana.
T: Very well. A banana would be ideal. It's 88 calories. But what's important is that it contains something very precious to you, potassium, alright?
P: Mmh, yes.
T: So how much is that? Let's do the maths together: 862 calories. I don't want to go straight to 1,400 calories – we'll get there slowly. It's enough to be over 1,000 calories because otherwise your body defends itself, OK? – *Using the "go slow" technique to avoid encouraging resistance* –

P: Mmh.
T: What do you like to have for dinner?
P: For example, one week meat, fish, one day ricotta ...
T: Very good, because so far we've added carbohydrates and sugars. Obviously, we need protein. Ricotta is perfect. But how many calories does ricotta have? Do you know?
P: No ...
T: Cow's milk ricotta has 146 calories per 100 grams ... it's a bit thin. For example, when you eat ricotta you should really eat 200 grams. The same is true when you eat white meat – 200 grams. Fish, 250. When you eat red meat, 150 grams. Can we do this?
P: Mmh, yes.
T: What kind of vegetables do you like best?
P: All of them.
T: Good. Some bread as well, or no bread?
P: I won't eat bread for now ...
T: It doesn't matter ... the important thing is that we follow these quantities, OK?
T: So I gave you a nutrition plan of 1,000 calories, 1,000–1,300 calories. This is perfect to start with. [Turning to the parents] You must avoid talking about her problem because when you talk about it, you feed it. Therefore, I'll ask you to take part in a sort of conspiracy of silence on your daughter's disorder. But you [talking to the mother] must respect the agreed nutrition scheme. Do you remember it? [They repeat the quantities] – *Prescriptions for parents: 1. Conspiracy of silence on the problem, 2. Observation without direct intervention, 3. Preparation of meals according to the agreed nutrition scheme* –
M: What about what she sees on the plate?
T: She made arrangements with me ... [turning to the patient] Right?
P: True.
T: And five lemon biscuits in the morning. But from now on you must absolutely avoid talking about food. Let's only talk about it when you come here, OK?
F AND M: Yes.
T: Good. I'll see you in two weeks.

During the first session, the therapist asks numerous discriminating strategic questions to assess the rigidity of the patient's pathological perceptive-reactive system and her motivation to change. Moreover, he obtains her collaboration to introduce an adequate meal plan for the recovery of her psychophysical well-being and of the agreed weight without resorting to eliciting the fear of forced-feeding in the hospital. The investigation of the social, familial, and school system reveals important factors that maintain and potentially aggravate the disorder. In fact, the patient has abandoned her studies and interrupted the sport she previously played at a competitive level. She has shut herself off by isolating herself except when she goes out with her parents and, in particular, when she does things with her mother. Therefore, a mother-daughter pathological complementary relationship has been established which helps to maintain the social closure of the girl and her difficult relationships with food and with herself.

Second session

T: How did things go over the past few weeks? – *Investigating the effects of the first session* –

P: A bit better than before. I couldn't keep to the full amount of pasta, all 100 grams. Breakfast is better, before I wasn't having it at all ... I also had a snack, although I've only eaten the banana once. I'm doing better, I'm doing a bit better.

T: And what effect has this had on your sensations? – *Strategically oriented question* –

P: The first time I had breakfast I was thinking "OK, I'll start with two biscuits, and slowly I'll work my way up to five". But I've eaten five biscuits since day one and I haven't felt dizzy so far ...

T: What a surprise! How weird!

P: So far, I've been able to do my activities.

T: And the following days?

P: Same thing. My head spins a little bit in the evening.

T: What did mum notice?

M: I've noticed that her panic attacks that were previously really frequent and scary, have vanished like magic ...

T: Like magic! [They laugh]

M: And whereas before, she was shaking in front of food, now she prepares her own plate herself and says: "I'll eat a little bit, because I don't want to have any problems". I didn't interfere, and I felt like a weight had been lifted. Your advice to "mind my own business" was excellent, because I hadn't known what to do anymore ...

T: Well, I didn't literally say "mind your own business" ...

M: Conspiracy of silence.

T: Good, observing without intervening, conspiracy of silence.

M: And I felt much calmer, because I used to talk too much and her anxiety only got worse when I talked too much.

T: So you're telling me that there has been a nice change over the past two weeks?

P: With the mirror as well: before, I'd always look at myself when I got dressed, but now I do it so rarely ...

T: And, can I ask, by increasing the amount that you ate, did you feel like you were exploding, becoming a disgusting ball of fat, or did you experience different sensations? – *Discerning strategic question* –
P: No ...
T: How did you feel?
P: Good.
T: OK, good. I must congratulate you for that big smile – it's so much brighter! You obviously can't see yourself but, compared to last time, there's a big difference when I look at you. And I think your mum can say the same, right? – *Positive reinforcement to encourage the achieved change* –
M: Mmh, yes.
T: Good. And how did you react to this change in the family? – *Investigating reactions to changes in the family system* –
M: Conspiracy of silence. [They laugh]
T: Hold everything! Let's not break the magic!
M: We've never made any comments, nothing ... Actually, she tends to tell me: "Mum, I tasted that, I did that" and I'll say: "You know, you made a deal with the professor, you know what to do. Think back to the session, decide for yourself whether you're doing the right things or not, I don't know anything".
P: In fact, at the beginning I thought: "Why isn't mum saying anything?!" [All smile]
T: How did mum keep quiet?
CT: She was feeling hurt by this silence!
T: You know what your friends could say, the ones who are a bit nasty? "Finally we've found someone to shut her up!" – *Using irony to reinforce the relationship* –
T: OK, and how was your life this week beyond food? Good? – *Investigating the area of school and social life* –
P: I left school. Still bad, basically.
T: Are you always very worried and scared? – *Strategic oriented questions* –
P: No, no, when I think about the future, I'm calmer.
T: Good.
P: That is, before, I felt like any mistake I made was unforgivable, like a death sentence, but now I can see that ... maybe ... I don't see it as a mistake but as a change, there's always something new.
T: This is very important, the fact that you can accept making mistakes, it's not a death sentence but an evolution ... Very good.

You know, the disorder that brought you here last time is like a suit of armour that can protect but also imprison. If you start breaking up the armour you'll realise that life can also be lived by committing transgressions, little mistakes that help us improve. That is, it turns out that a small mistake is not a death sentence but a step back that allows us to take two steps forward; it's that obstacle that lets us discover that we can regain our balance

and that, if it wasn't there, it wouldn't give us the opportunity to develop confidence in ourselves and in our ability to overcome things. Good, good. Did you weigh yourself? — *Restructuring the possibility of making mistakes to reinforce the change that has taken place in the patient's perception* —
P: No …
T: Were you afraid to, or weren't you doing it systematically in the first place? — *Discerning strategic question* —
P: I never do it.
T: And when you looked at yourself in the mirror, did you see yourself as fat? — *Discerning strategic question* —
P: No, that only happens rarely.
T: Ok, I'm very happy …
P: By the way, a couple of times I saw myself as skinny.
T: This deserves an explanation, you know? I'll give you an example: when I treat girls who are in really life-threatening situations who come in here weighing 28–29 kilograms, the paradox is that, as long as they're dangerously underweight, they seem themselves as fat. In the session I'll tell them: "When you're about 45 kilograms, you'll see yourself as very thin" and they'll say: "That's nonsense, Professor!" Then they reach 45 kilograms and, right on schedule, they discover that I was right! Because the trap of anorexia is precisely this dysmorphophobic effect on our perception. If you start eating again like you have been, you will look in the mirror and see yourself strangely thin; therefore, the recovery of an accurate perception will happen in conjunction with the maintenance of this course. I don't want to increase anything right now. I want you to keep doing what we've already established. Then, depending on how you feel, we'll adjust it. Also because, as we've already said, a girl like you, with your body structure, should eat around 1,400 calories per day, no less, no more, enjoying life, food, and everything else, OK? So at the moment the important thing is that we consolidate what we've achieved, and then we'll move forward by taking small steps, but I want to tell you that you've already taken the most important step. You've done half the job. Now let's keep it up, OK? — *Use of explanatory language to explain the dysmorphophobic effects of restrictive eating and to support and consolidate the change achieved* —
P: Yes.
M: Yes.
T: I'll see you in two weeks.

Between the first and the second session, important changes have occurred in the patient, both in her relationship with food and with herself. In fact, the recovery of a healthier nutrition was associated with the attenuation of dysmorphophobia, mood improvement, and anxiety reduction. In addition, her perfectionist attitude has softened so much that the girl is able to consider the possibility of a mistake with serenity and see it as an incentive for personal growth. The prescriptions given to the parents have stopped some of their behaviours that fed the disorder; this has provided relief for both the daughter and the parents themselves, in particular for the mother, who was more enmeshed in the relationship with the daughter.

Third session

T: So, what's new? How've you been these past two weeks? – *Investigating the effects of the first session –*
P: Better than I felt before …
T: Even better?
P: Yes, I feel better than the previous weeks …
T: Very good … And what's making you feel better, in your opinion? – *Strategically oriented question –*
P: I'm calmer, truly much calmer.
T: Good. Is mum also noticing this?
M: Yes, yes … I see that she's more communicative, more extroverted than she was before, less closed.
T: Mmh, and what are you doing differently in your everyday life now that you feel calmer? – *Redefining by using evocative analogic language –*
P: Maybe, if I have to make decisions or go out with my friends, I'm more willing to do it … I'm less passive.
T: Less closed up inside the armour that had become a prison.
M: Yes, in every way … She's also more careful with her little brother; she takes better care of him.
T: Do you still feel as though you're wearing the armour, or have we broken it? – *Discerning strategic question –*
P: It's still there …
T: And this armour, that before was a prison and is now just armour, how does it show itself? – *Strategically oriented question –*
P: Well, for example, sometimes when I look at myself, it's like the armour's still telling me: "You're huge". But other times it immediately tells me: "that's not true", and everything passes.
T: Good.
P: Other times I start crying … I have crying spells.
T: How do you usually see yourself in the mirror now? Very big? Huge? Or do you see yourself in a more balanced way? – *Discerning strategic question –*
P: A bit better.
T: So how do you see yourself?
P: Sometimes when I have a problem I go to my mum and ask her if I'm the only one who sees myself like this …
T: Ah, so you only wear the magnifying lenses occasionally … that's the famous armour. Good, we're really pleased. Really. And you're smiling

even more ... [Speaking to the parents] So, are you also noticing these changes? — *Positive reinforcement to change* —
M: Yes, yes ... she's much calmer, less anxious. Before, she sometimes needed to just get out, all of a sudden, she'd have to get out, because she felt the house was closing in around her ... But now she's calmer.
T: Have you been able to respect our agreements about food? — *Investigating the agreed daily food regime* —
P: Half of the pasta ...
T: Does "half of the pasta" mean that you haven't eaten the agreed amount?
P: Yes.
T: And was this like a rebellion against the idea, or was there some other reason? — *Discerning strategic question* —
P: I don't know ... I was already full.
T: Good. And what does your body say, not in the mirror but on the weighing scales?[11] — *Strategically oriented question* —
P: I don't know.
M: She doesn't weigh herself.
T: Yes, I remember ... I just wanted to check if this time she felt like doing it.
M: I checked her blood pressure and it's slightly improved. Before it was 90/60, now it's 106/67. She still gets dizzy in the evening, though.
T: What do your clothes tell us? You know your sizes.
P: They're always the same.
CT: Have you tried the variant of putting a thin layer of jam on toast in the morning?
P: No, I still haven't ...
T: Still too risky?
P: It's like I'm making some habits ... For example, I always have breakfast in the morning with the same cup.
T: So you tend to set standards in everything you do, don't you? Once you do something in a certain way, you repeat it in the same way, always the same ...
P: Yes.
M: Even if she doesn't go to school in the morning, she wants to come with me because she refuses to stay at home by herself, in case she goes into a panic. And when it's breakfast time, she'll ask me, "can I have breakfast?" ... and then she has it.
T: So at the moment you're refusing to eat pasta?
P: I eat half of it.
M: In the beginning she was checking the quantity of olive oil in the pasta, though now she understands that pasta doesn't taste good without olive oil, and she lets me do it.
T: Absolutely!
M: Yes, she only let me use olive oil once ... then she tried it without oil and thought it was disgusting and she's eaten it with the olive oil since!

T: OK. But you know we can't afford the risk of a step backwards. So I agree with you eating half of the pasta. For example, I don't exactly love pasta ... I'm one of the few Italians who hardly ever eats pasta – but then you have to eat something else ... – *Reference to compliance and adherence to agreed nutritional indications* –

P: Is it OK if I eat a slice of bread in the evening?

T: All right then. If you eat a slice of bread in the evening, that's fine. You found the solution by yourself ... Look, you say that now you've started going out with your friends a little bit, right? How do you feel about that? Do you feel transparent around them, or do they really see you?[12] – *Discerning strategic question* –

P: No, I'm more present. Just yesterday I was told by a friend that I'm different now, more present ...

T: I explained to you that your problem isn't just with food. One abstains from everything and everyone. In fact, the way out isn't only through eating, but also through discovering all the pleasant sensations, especially relationships with others; and having social contact with others should become a daily routine for you. Could you do that, or don't you feel like doing it? – *Restructuring aimed at encouraging the recovery of relationships with peers* –

P: Before, I was going to school, but it's harder now. I only see them when they have time.

T: But just keep in touch. You must keep in touch with them every day. This is extremely important. – *Creating an agreement to establish daily contacts with peers* –

P: Yes, I'm doing that, yes.

T: Very good ...

T: Another question: what do you intend to do about school? – *Strategic discerning question* –

P: I still ... don't feel like it.

T: Would it be too destabilising for you?

P: Yes.

T: OK, it was just a question, not an order. The important thing is that you keep in touch with your classmates and your friends. But do you think that in the future you'll go back to school?

P: I don't know ... I need more time.

T: We'll come back to this. There's no hurry. What's important is to continue what we're doing with food, because this is what broke the prison and allowed us to make a chink in the armour, and relationships with others are part of the anti-armour. All right? – *Using the go slow technique to avoid encouraging resistance and to promote the strengthening of the achieved goals* –

P: I wanted to say that every day I play some volleyball in the school gym where mum works ...

T: On your own?

P: Yes.
T: For how long?
P: Only a couple of shots ...
T: You can play for half an hour.
P: No, only a couple of shots.
T: Of course, you can take a couple of shots.
P: Good.
T: I'll see you in two weeks.

The break of the perceptive-reactive anorexic system is highlighted not only by food consumption but also by the patient's interest in relationships with peers, which are experienced with pleasure. Now therefore, daily contact with friends is encouraged. At the same time, perceptions, emotions, and intentions regarding school drop-out are explored, without intervening directly to urge recovery. In fact, by promoting and reinforcing the results achieved, the girl herself will perceive going back to school as appropriate and desired.

Fourth session

T: So, what's new? How did you spend these past few weeks? — *Investigating the change process: nutrition, relationship with herself, relationship with others* —
P: Some days I've been feeling a bit lost — maybe because I'm not going to school ... I'm waiting for my course to start so that I can be busy again — and other days I'm starting to like myself ...
T: Oh ... can you describe that in more detail?
P: I look in the mirror and I don't see myself as a balloon ... I see myself as normal.
T: So, some days the mirror isn't magnified and magnifying and when you look at yourself you think, "But ... I'm pretty!" How's your relationship with the outside world? — *Redefining with use of analogical language* —
P: When I can't see my friends, I call them.
T: Is there a boyfriend or are you still abstaining from dating?
P: There's still no-one ...
T: Did you make progress with our food agreement?
P: The first week I couldn't eat bread. However, in the last few days I managed it. I really felt the need for the bread as well as the side dish because I was still feeling dizzy in the evening.
T: What does the weighing scale tell us?
P: I don't weigh myself ...
T: You don't want to weigh yourself, but the mirror is telling us that you're seeing yourself better. What does mum say?

M: I wish she would start to live in her own dimension. Because currently she's coming into work with me. We're both living half a life. She should live her own life.
T: That's asking too much for now. — *Redefining with the use of the "go slow" technique* —
M: Oh, then we'll wait.
T: Have you reached what we'd agreed as a nutrition plan?
M: She's weighing out 50 grams of pasta, is that right?
CT: That's right. [The mother apologises to her daughter]
T: Was it difficult for you to respect the agreement or did it go pretty well? — *Discerning strategic question* —
P: It went well.
T: Good. So do you think this is the right course or not? — *Discerning strategic question* —
P: The right one!
T: So you feel that this is the right way ... When your mum says: "I'd like everyone to live their own lives rather than half a life", how does that affect you? — *Strategically oriented question* —
P: It's true ... this is weighing on me. I feel like I don't belong there ... That's her job and I ...
T: And when your mum says to you: "I'd prefer it if you didn't always come with me", do you think you'd be able to do something about it, or is it too early, as I said? — *Discerning strategic question* —
P: If my course starts, that is, if they accept my application, then I'll do something else.
T: So, you're saying: "If the course starts, I'll be busy, and then I can stop going with my mum" ... So you can do it!
CT: What course is it?
P: Baking ...
T: Hmm, what a coincidence ... So you'll become very good at making cakes.
M: She's already good ...
T: Would you attend the course every day?
P: No, three times a week. You get a certificate. It lasts two months ...
T: Good, so you can dedicate the rest of the time to your own life ... And let's see if some boyfriend turns up ... [Speaking to the mother] Mum, have you noticed whether she has any admirers?
M: She should hang out with more people ... I don't see any admirers on the horizon for now ... But there's nothing wrong with her.
T: Is that a question or a statement? This is part of her disorder because, you see, she sees herself as anything but beautiful. She sees herself as a monster that no-one could like. And even if someone liked her, it would mean that this person must have much worse problems ... isn't that right? [The patient nods] The majority of girls who have this problem are clearly

good-looking, beautiful, but they see themselves as the opposite. – *Restructuring to tune in with the patient's own perception –*
M: But she's always had this insecurity, even when she was studying. She could recite the whole lesson by heart but she never felt ready ...
T: If we're talking about attractiveness and desirability, not feeling liked is even worse.
M: [Speaking to her daughter] Haven't I said that there are girls who aren't as pretty as you who go around all cocky, and they're nowhere near as good-looking as you ... But you ... Why don't you appreciate yourself?
T: Please, avoid telling her this, OK? – *Blocking mother's attempted dysfunctional solutions –*
M: Yes, I've stopped ... I used to say that.
T: Good. We'll be very happy if you start this course, but even if this isn't possible, you'll find other activities that you like or that interest you, OK? And let's keep to what we have agreed upon ... Please remember! Alright? – *Positive reinforcement and incentive to maintain therapeutic agreements –*
P: Yes, yes.

The improvements in the girl's relationship with food, in her self-perception, and in her social relationships have been maintained and strengthened. Moreover, the desire for an independent life distinct from that of her mother is beginning to emerge. Therefore, she is not directly prescribed to stop sharing most days with her mother, but she is stimulated to engage in more activities chosen according to her interests.

Fifth session

T: So, how did you spend the past two weeks? Have you started the bakery course? – *Investigating the change process: sense of self, relationships, social life –*
P: I like it because I feel more independent; I really wanted to go on the course ... as if I needed it ...
T: Very good. And how are things going with other people?
P: Well.
T: So no-one's treating you like you were the one that left?
P: What?
T: I mean, nobody sees that you have a problem?
P: No, no.
T: And do you behave like someone who doesn't have any problems, or do you still feel fragile and like you need to defend yourself? – *Discerning strategic question –*
P: No, I'm really more open ...
T: And from the point of view of your appearance, do you feel calmer or not? – *Discerning strategic question –*

88 Appendix

P: No … It's as if, when I look at myself with my own eyes, I see myself as ugly, kind of fat, chubby … Instead, if I look at myself through other people's eyes, it's the opposite.

T: And what's that?

P: Pretty. It's like I have a problem with it.

T: Look, whose are the most suitable eyes? Yours or theirs? – *Discerning strategic question –*

P: Theirs.

T: For people who are going through or have gone through your problem there's a phase in which the suggestion we give is precisely this: to look with other people's eyes, because they are more realistic and more reliable than your own. Your eyes have deforming lenses that always make you look fat and encourage you to restrict. You must wear other people's lenses. This is good … this is really good. – *Restructuring to encourage functional behaviour –*

T: [Speaking to the mother] What does mum say?

M: Yes, I can see that she's much calmer. [The girl cries]

T: These are beautiful tears … There is a splendid Indian idiom of tears that turn into pearls when one comes through suffering, pain, and sacrifice. – *Restructuring with the use of analogue language –*

M: When she goes to the course, she's calm and she's also made friends with another girl who she hung out with and who she immediately exchanged phone numbers with. Before, that would have been impossible! Instead, when she comes with me in the morning, I can see that she's confused, suffering …

T: I'd say that now you can stop doing it, right?

M: Hmm … It's just that she says she's afraid to face breakfast alone …

T: Yes, but wait, you could have breakfast with mum before she leaves. Then we'll begin to take care of the jewel that turns tears into pearls because if you continue to go to the school with her, to help and be helped, you keep telling yourself: you're sick. We must make sure that you manage yourself, that you're independent. However, now it's the holidays … – *Restructuring by using explanatory and analogical language to interrupt dysfunctional behaviour –*

M: Yes, tomorrow we're going to visit her grandparents …

T: Good. As soon as you get back from holiday I'd like you to start staying at home, OK? You've got to start organising your day while you wait for the course to start, without mum, so that you loosen this cord and make sure that you become independent and autonomous. Call your friends, call whoever you want, instead of going with mum. So let's keep going with everything we have achieved, because I see you doing well. Now what's left to do is to use other people's eyes, and to add a relationship with the outside world. In the morning you can go out, see people, call them … OK? You can have breakfast together, then you go back to bed

and she goes to work. Do you think you can do that, or am I asking too much? – *Prescriptions: 1. Maintaining the achieved results, 2. In the relationship with the outside world, rely on the perception of others with respect to their aesthetic judgment of the patient, 3. Interrupting the mother-daughter pathogenic complementarity* –
P: No ... no ... I can do it.
T: And mum must be able to leave without fearing the worst, OK?
M: It's just that she feels dizzy in the mornings ...
T: In fact, that's the reason why you'll have breakfast together, and then you'll go to work while your daughter takes care of her appearance and takes care of herself, OK?
M: OK ...

The process of change has seen progressive improvements on a personal and interpersonal level, so much so that the need for self-affirmation is now emerging. Therefore, in this phase, it is possible to intervene directly to block the behaviours that continue to feed the mother–daughter pathological complementarity, as this hinders the girl's path of emancipation and growth.

Sixth session

T: How have you felt over this period? How did you spend your days? – *Investigating the change process* –
P: Everything's fading away. When I look at myself in the mirror I can really see myself and I don't say: "I'm fat", anymore, like when I was looking at myself before ... that is, when I'm tired, the fear comes back, but the feeling is different ... the distorting aura is gone ...
T: The aura is gone ... what a strange thing, eh? How can you explain it? – *Strategically oriented question* –
P: For me this is magic! Before, nothing was changing!
T: But this aura is gone ... if you think about it, what have we made you change since we met you? – *Strategically oriented question* –
P: Eating food ... above all ...
T: Very good. And there's no magic, OK? We made you do things that you were afraid of doing, but it was you who broke the negative spell and replaced the magnifying lenses with appropriate lenses ... so you did the magic; we only led you to put it into practice. So, how do you see yourself now with clear eyes? Are you ugly and fat or are you pretty? – *Restructuring using analogical and explanatory language to highlight the patient's resources and to assign the responsibility of the change to her* –
P: Pretty ... [She smiles]
T: Very good. You know that since the second appointment we've seen you grow more and more beautiful and bright and we see you improving each

time, and this makes us so proud and happy. And what's changed in your life without this veil? – *Positive reinforcement to change* –
P: I've got more freedom – it's as if I've really started living ... That's to say, there's more freedom in everything.
T: And you remember that last time we talked about an important topic concerning being your mum's assistant and how this means that you need assistance ... have you kept doing that or not? – *Discerning strategic question* –
P: Yeah, sometimes, other times I stayed at home, and sometimes I went there later.
T: Very good ...
M: She stayed in bed, she never did that before. Now she gets up when she goes to school, she gets up to take the train ...
T: Good. In your opinion, in the next few weeks will you still have to go with her sometimes or can you stay at home? – *Discerning strategic question* –
P: I don't know ...
T: We said: "If you behave like an assistant, you need assistance" ... So let's get rid of this mutual assistance, OK? – *Restructuring to elicit aversion towards dysfunctional behaviour* –
And when you're out and about and you look at other people, how do you feel they look at you? Do you feel rejected or judged, or do you feel liked and appreciated? – *Discerning strategic question* –
P: No, it disappears around other people ... Nobody notices that I have a problem.
T: So they just appreciate you for who you are?
P: Yes.
T: So are you communicating with others, are you having social contact?
P: Yes, yes ... I feel good with other people.
T: This makes us even more happy and proud. And this is the path to add now: more social contact, more availability in contact and interaction, and completely cutting off that dependency on your mum, OK? – *Positive reinforcement emphasising the previous indications* –
P: Now when I go to school on my own, I feel like I'm in those American movies where you see a lady walking down the street with a cappuccino in her hand ... I feel like that: totally free.
T: Very good ... You're using other people's eyes while yours are gradually refining. That's great, let's proceed. From now until next week, we'd like you to stop being an assistant and being assisted, and we want you to continue to see yourself through other people's eyes, OK? Is mum calm?
M: Yes ... very ... Yesterday she made a cake and sold it!
T: As you can see, no magic ... You are the magic person, if you give yourself the chance to express yourself. – *Using evocative language to highlight the patient's resources* –

In this phase of the therapy, the goals achieved are becoming stable and they promote the development of a functional balance. This is also highlighted by the remission of the dysmorphophobic perceptions. Therefore, it becomes increasingly important to ensure that the patient acquires full awareness and confidence in her own resources, also through the attribution of responsibility for the changes in the therapeutic process.

Seventh session

CT: How did you spend the last few days? How have you been? — *Investigating the change process* —

P: More peaceful. Some days I asked my mum to tell me how I really am, and some days I told her what I have clear in my mind … what I want to do: I want to learn languages and start playing volleyball again.

T: So you've had a flash of inspiration these past few weeks. And have you started doing something about it or are you still waiting? — *Discerning strategic question* —

P: I have to finish the bakery course first, and then I want to combine the two.

T: Very good. Have you tried to make eye contact with people that you don't know and smile at them instead of looking down? — *Discerning strategic question* —

P: Yes.

T: And have you seen that people reject you or are they nice to you?

P: No, they're nice. People tell me I'm beautiful, and the ones who already knew me are happy because I'm recovering and they compliment me so much; but sometimes what they say makes me think I'm getting fat …

T: People are nice because you make them feel good and important first. You know that seeing beautiful eyes makes everyone feel good. It should be a social medicine shared with everyone … — *Restructuring* —

M: Smiles are an open door to heaven.

T: Exactly … and then beautiful eyes and a beautiful smile like yours are better than paradise! And if you give a gift to others, what comes back to you is much more than what you gave them. Try to bear that in mind, don't forget it. The more you make others feel important, the more everyone's happy, because you'll feel better too. It's not an act of altruism but of healthy selfishness, because it's a constructive interaction. But then, if they tell you that you look fine, you think: "I got fat!" — *Restructuring* —

P: Yes, someone I hadn't seen for a long time told me that.

T: And did you think: "I got fat and I have to lose weight", or: "OK, I'm fine like this"? — *Discerning strategic question* —

P: Sometimes I thought: "OK, I'm fine".

T: Last time we said that you needed to learn to use the eyes of others to be able to use yours. [Speaking to her mother] Mum, how do you see her?

M: Better. She told me that she wanted to take up volleyball again in September. I told her that she'll have to get back in physical condition to be able to perform with the team at her best. If you go back, you have to go back healthy, since you stopped because of these problems. There were a few moments of panic where she asked for reassurance and others where she was calmer. All in all, she's doing well.

T: And how did you organise your days, did you stay at home or did you go in with her? – *Discerning strategic question* –

P: I mostly stayed at home. Sometimes I went out with dad.

M: Yes, if she was coming with me, later she would be going out and doing her own things. She met up with her high school and theatre friends. Then there was the birthday party. She turned 18 and celebrated with her friends and she stayed out all evening without covering her shoulders!

T: Well, you've found the people you had left behind ...

P: Yes.

M: She's also more careful and attentive towards her brother and the dogs.

T: Good ... very good, I'm really happy. And will you see those guys again soon?

P: Yes, yes.

T: So from now until next time let's continue along the same road. If you spend time with people, you'll see that everything will improve spontaneously. See you in three weeks.

The girl is gaining a greater sense of security and she is increasingly improving her management of social contact, even interactions with strangers. She is gradually starting to accept her body and to outline sport and schoolwork goals that she intends to achieve. Therefore, it was decided to leave more time between sessions to allow the patient to strengthen the results achieved alone and to mobilise her personal resources.

Eighth session

CT: How did this month go? – *Investigating the change process* –

P: Much better.

CT: Much better, really! Can you describe what you mean?

P: It's as if it's almost done! As if I'm very close to healing completely. Sometimes I'll hit a small roadblock, where I start not eating very much. Like last time I didn't feel well with my stomach, that mechanism was coming back ...

CT: Did you restrict your nutritional intake a little?

P: Yes ... mmh ... But then the rest ... social contact with others ... All of that's fine.

T: So you went out. Did you see your school and theatre friends?
P: The theatre group not so much; I mostly saw the people from school.
CT: So has the baking course not finished yet?
P: Not yet.
T: And when did you have these moments where you felt like restricting your eating? Did they come from nowhere or did they perhaps follow having seen someone who told you that you looked good, as you said last time, and this alerted you to your weight? – *Discerning strategic question* –
P: No, maybe I felt nauseous, I didn't digest food properly or I didn't want to eat and then that mechanism came back. But I'm also starting to eat with other people. I ate without cooking separately for myself. This is what's happening now ... before, I couldn't do that.
M: Before, we absolutely had to weigh everything. Now she's more flexible about weighing food and she eats with others!
T: I see! So are you happy with this situation or are you a bit worried? – *Discerning strategic question* –
P: No.
T: No worries?
P: No, I'll be glad if I continue like this.
T: What does mum say?
M: Mum is much calmer because now, she's chatting to a boy and she's staying awake until 2 am on the phone!
T: Oh, good! Where did you get the boy from?
P: School ...
T: But had you already noticed him?
P: No ... Let's say he spoke up!
T: So you noticed him and you managed to seduce him! With those beautiful eyes ... you properly beguiled him! Very good, we're very happy, you know? And this is the strongest antagonist to your disorder: when a person manages to enjoy not only the pleasure of food, but also the pleasure of social contact and intimate relationships. [Speaking to the mother] What are mum's concerns?
M: No, no concerns ... She's calm and she must live this moment that I consider to be an excellent lifebelt. Then, what will be will be ... Before, she was so shy and always asking me: "Mum, can I live this moment?". Under normal circumstances she shouldn't even ask this; a person should do it secretly, without asking for permission. She thought she'd always stay with us, but it's not like that.
T: We're very happy, so let's proceed. We have nothing to add: you just have to discover your sensations. This time we'll meet again after the summer break, so you have the chance to really experience this moment.

The girl has reached one of the most feared goals of those suffering from eating disorders. That is, eating with other people. She has also abandoned her obsessive control over food as she is now able to weigh portions with her eyes instead of weighing quantities on the scale. At the same time, she can eat food cooked by others. She has also established a romantic relationship with a boy that she is experiencing with pleasure, and she shows satisfaction with her achievements.

Ninth session

CT: How've you been these past two summer months? – *Investigating the change process* –
P: Everything went fine during the holidays, school started again ... and, OK, just some panic attacks. I've started playing volleyball again and I felt lost among my teammates, and I panicked.
T: Panic or fear?
P: Real panic.
T: Panic means: "Oh my God, I can't do it, oh God, I'm stuck, I have to run away".
P: Eh, yes.
T: But did you get over it or did you run away and interrupt what you were doing? – *Discerning strategic question* –
P: No, no ...
T: So it wasn't panic, it was a fear that you overcame. Panic is when one is paralysed; fear can also be strong but if you overcome it or if you stay there to face the situation, it's not panic. OK, so you're facing all the things you had escaped from; it's normal that at the beginning this scares you. – *Restructuring* –
How's school going? Is it going well?
P: Well.
T: Is the boyfriend still there?
P: No ...
T: Oh ... Did he disappear or did you dump him?
P: Oh well ... we were different ...
T: You realised that it wasn't working.
M: Let's say that he disappeared, but then she realised that they were different ...
T: What's mum seeing?
M: That she's maturing a lot and she's starting to deal with things, even if sometimes there are these residual panic attacks that she brilliantly overcomes ...
T: So, there are moments of anxiety or fear ... The important thing is to look fear in the eye, because it'll turn into courage. If you run away, it becomes panic. The important thing is to fight those moments. If you give up, you're defeated; if you go ahead, you win. – *Restructuring aimed at encouraging functional behaviour* –

P: Going back? No way, not now!
T: If you give up, you're defeated; if you go ahead, you win. Have the old problems ever come back?
P: Some fear of my body, but not like before.
T: How do you see yourself now?
P: Let's say well, but there are moments when I tell mum that I feel enormous.
T: What does mum say?
M: Mum yells at her to stop joking because now she's truly reached physical beauty, the kind she wanted and, also, other people are noticing it and telling her: "you look good" ... Sometimes someone will use hellish terminology and tell her: "you've put on weight", and she goes haywire, but then she realises that it was only an expression, that she's not really huge. She's facing other people's comments now, before there was total shutting down ...
T: But when you look at yourself in the mirror without clothes, how do you see yourself? Fat or fit? – *Discerning strategic question* –
P: My legs are a bit disproportionate compared to the rest of me, but then I say: "No, it's not like that".
T: And when you see them as disproportionate – muscular, because you're training them now – do you think they're actually like that or do you think it depends on your old deforming lenses? – *Discerning strategic question* –
P: I think ..."Oh well, so they're fat, it doesn't matter!" I don't care about this! [They laugh]
T: How's the comparison with your female friends going?
P: I haven't played for two years, so ...
T: No, not on performance, on beauty ... Do you see them as more good-looking than you, in better shape than you, or does the comparison make you understand that you're not so bad yourself? – *Discerning strategic question* –
P: No, no, I don't think about this.
T: Ok, so you think about your performance, about how good you are?
P: Yes, because I'm a bit behind on the court.
T: What's your typical day like now?
P: Busier ... For example, yesterday I came back very late ... Yesterday, after school, I attended a course to get my food hygiene certificate, I went back home, and then immediately went off to play volleyball!
T: Is mum calm or worried about this separation?
M: No, no [they laugh] ... Mum really needs it! I tell her she should go abroad!
T: [Speaking to the mother] Before, she was always stuck to you!
M: She's old enough now and I want to see her become autonomous.
T: She's becoming so. We're really glad and impressed.

CT: Are you continuing with the baking course in the mornings then?
P: Yes!
T: She'll bring us a cake when she's professional! [They laugh]
T: See you in three months. We'll add a month each time …
P: On Sunday I start an internship with my professor.
T: Cooking?
P: No, as a waitress!
CT: Good, that's how we all start out! Small steps for big endeavours.

The patient has resumed all the activities that she interrupted during the pathology, volleyball included. The comparison with her teammates at the level of athletic performance has aroused fear and initial demoralisation. However, she has overcome this as she has continued her practice sessions with commitment. Although some parts of her body are still perceived as huge and disharmonious compared to the rest of the body, her reaction to this was not typical of anorexia, for example suffering, non-acceptance, and eating restriction, but rather was a healthy indifference.

Tenth session

R: So, what do you tell us about this long period? – *Investigating the change process: eating, social contact, self-image* –
P: I feel better, calmer. With my appearance, sometimes I see myself as overweight again, but I'm living more freely and if I want an extra biscuit in the evening, after practice, I have one.
T: Good, good …
P: Yes, I'll eat an extra something if I'm hungrier …
T: And do you allow yourself to do that with no qualms, or do you worry about this? – *Discerning strategic question* –
P: No, I allow myself to do it freely. I'm even waking up less frequently at night.
M: She's active during the day and she sleeps during the night.
T: OK, how's life going outside of home?
P: I'm still going to school and I'm playing volleyball three times a week.
T: Very good.
P: Since the last session, school and volleyball …
T: Good. Is there a boyfriend?
P: Not yet.
T: Are we keeping them away?
P: Mmh.
T: Do you hang out with friends or are you quite isolated?
P: Yes, yes, I usually hang out with friends … It's the Christmas holidays soon, we'll be all free, so …
T: Do you go out?

P: No, not in the evening.
T: OK. Not even Saturdays and Sundays? Never?
P: On Sundays I go to watch games at the gym and on Saturdays sometimes I go out with my family or sometimes with friends.
T: Perfect ... [Speaking to the mother] What does mum say?
M: I see that she's calmer, much more relaxed in when it comes to adversity. Before, she'd get hysterical, now she seems much more composed, more reasonable in dealing with problems.
T: Is mum's evaluation that there is still a disorder, or not anymore?
M: No.
T: [Speaking to the patient] OK, now the same question to you: do you think you still have the disorder or have your difficulties been completely overcome? — *Discerning strategic question* —
P: No, not a real disorder, but I still don't have much self-confidence ...
T: But, you know, self-confidence isn't a gift, it's a conquest, and it's conquered by experience and by having more and more success and more trust in your own resources. — *Restructuring* —
Good, good. And what do you think we need to do to increase your self-confidence?
P: Mmh.
T: Should we add something or just keep to the route you're following? — *Strategically oriented question* —
P: No, it's OK like this.
T: Very good. I agree too. It's just a matter of strengthening the results achieved so far over time.
P: For example, there are about 20 girls on the volleyball team ... There was one girl in particular who I never talked to before because, I don't know, we didn't like each other, but now I talk to her, too. I feel more part of the team ... And I've started talking to everyone lately, even people who I instinctively didn't get along with at the beginning ... And we talk about everything, school, boys ...
T: Of course, all the things girls talk about! Including secrets and things that we shouldn't know ... [They laugh]
T: Good, I'm really happy. This time we'll meet again in six months and it'll be the second to last time that we'll see each other, if all goes according to plan, OK? Then we'll meet again after another six months and we'll check everything.

At the first follow-up, three months after the previous session, the objectives had stabilised, allowing the girl to express new perceptive-emotional, cognitive, and behavioural repertoires which are functional to her well-being and growth. It is also important to evaluate the patient's and mother's experiences in relation to the overcoming of the pathology and/

or the presence of other forms of discomfort. Since the therapist's evaluation was consistent with those of the girl and the mother, the final appointments for six months' and one year's time were scheduled. In the last session, the girl arrived with a big decorated cake and a bottle of orange juice and invited the therapist and co-therapist to share them with her and her mother to celebrate an important victory of her team and the fact that she now feels free from the prison of anorexia and the trap of insecurity.

Notes

1. The discerning strategic questions, placed in the early phases of the assessment, allow the therapist to distinguish the patient's different perceptive-reactive systems when faced by the problem, providing indications of the diagnosis-intervention process that should be followed.
2. Questions with an illusion of alternative response are used to therapeutically direct the patient's response.
3. Besides elimination or compensation mechanisms such as vomiting, elimination, or exercising, among the most frequent acts that characterise the eating behaviour of people with anorexia are: chewing food for a while and then spitting it out, cutting food into increasingly smaller pieces, attempts to hide food under the plate, in napkins, or into their pockets, and eating very slowly.
4. With this redefinition, we want to clarify the hierarchical position of parents towards a minor daughter with a pathology. In this way, parents are stimulated to acquire behaviour that furthers the therapeutic process. Left alone in her relationship with the weighing scale, the patient, like the majority of anorexic patients in the early stages of therapy, would not report the correct weight; she would report an overestimation to minimise the threat of hospitalisation that she wants so desperately to avoid.
5. This question explores an important area of clinical interest related to which ways of increasing food intake are perceived as less threatening by the patient. This allows the therapist to be on the same page as her and to reach an agreement on the new daily regimen of meals.
6. These questions allow the therapist to discern whether the anorexic perceptive-reactive system has started its re-structuring process or not. It is important that when new foods are included, fear and rejection soon give way to a sense of tranquillity and pleasure.
7. This question, by extending the patient's assessment to her relational, social, and scholastic life, allows the therapist to obtain further indications on the therapeutic process already realised and of what is still to be achieved.
8. In this case, this form of double bind is used to maintain a warm and welcoming relationship with the patient that includes being directive and controlling the behaviours related to the pathology, which is metaphorically called "the other part of you".
9. This question extends the diagnostic assessment to areas of life beyond the relationship with food in order to detect limiting factors and incentivising the patient's healing process.
10. With these strategically oriented questions, family processes that probably contributed to the formation of the disorder as possible triggers are evaluated.

11 This question is aimed at further testing changes in the anorexic perceptive-reactive system. In fact, the initial improvements concerning nutrition and bodily sensations are often viewed with concern, as a threat, and can therefore re-trigger obsessive weight control and mechanisms of compensation and elimination of food from the diet.
12 In the therapeutic process, particular attention must be paid to patients' experiences in interpersonal relationships. These are often sources of considerable discomfort and suffering which find, in anorexia, a way to be attenuated, thus reinforcing eating restriction with numbness and the related perceptual-emotional detachment.

Bibliography

Alexander, F. (1946). *Psychoanalytic therapy: Principles and application*. New York, NY: Ronald Press.
American Psychiatric Association. (2013). *Diagnostic and statistical manual of mental disorders* (5th edition). Washington, DC: Author.
Ball, J., Mitchell, P. (2004). A randomized controlled study of cognitive behavior therapy and behavioral family therapy for anorexia nervosa patients. *Brunner-Mazel Eating Disorders Monograph Series*, 12, 303–314.
Biondi, M., Loriedo, C. (2011). *Disturbi di personalità. Identità e conflitti in una società in trasformazione*. Milan, IT: FrancoAngeli.
Casiero, D., Frishman, W.H. (2006). Cardiovascular complications of eating disorders. *Cardiology in Review*, 14, 227–231.
Castelnuovo, G., Manzoni, G.M., Villa, V., Cesa, G.L., Molinari, E. (2010). Brief strategic therapy vs cognitive behavioral therapy for the inpatient and telephone-based outpatient treatment of binge eating disorder: The STRATOB randomized controlled clinical trial. *Clinical Practice & Epidemiology in Mental Health: CP & EMH*, 7, 29.
Castelnuovo, G., Molinari, E., Nardone, G., Salvini, A. (2019). Empirical research in psychotherapy. In G. Nardone & A. Salvini (Eds.) *International dictionary of psychotherapy*. London, UK: Routledge.
Costa, E., Nazzaro, F., Vona, L. (2011). Trattamento integrato del DCA in comorbidità con i disturbi di personalità. In M. Biondi & C. Loriedo (Eds.) *Disturbi di personalità. Identità e conflitti in una società in trasformazione*. Milan, IT: FrancoAngeli.
Costa, M.B., Melnik, T. (2016). Effectiveness of psychosocial interventions in eating disorder: An overview of Cochrane systematic reviews. *Einstein*, 14(2), 235–277.
Cotugno, A., Benedetto, A. M. (1995). *Il paziente borderline. Introduzione clinica alla "patologia marginale"*. Milano: Franco Angeli.
Dalle Grave, R. (2015). *Alle mie pazienti dico … Informazione e auto-aiuto per superare i disturbi dell'alimentazione* (XV edition). Verona, IT: Positive Press.
Dare, C., Eisler, I. (1997). *Handbook of treatment for eating disorders*. New York, NY: Guilford Press.
Doidge, N. (2016). *The brain's way of healing: Remarkable discoveries and recoveries from the frontiers of neuroplasticity*. London, UK: Penguin Books.
Eisler, I., Dare, C., Hodes, M., Russell, G., Dodge, E., Le Grange, D. (2000). Family therapy for adolescent anorexia nervosa: The results of a controlled comparison of two family interventions. *Journal of Child Psychology and Psychiatry*, 41, 727–736.

Bibliography

Elkaim, M. (1995). *Panorama des thérapie familiales*. Paris, FR: Sueil.
Faravelli, C. (2010). *Psicofarmacologia per psicologi*. Bologna, IT: Il Mulino.
Favaro, A., Ferrara, S., Santnastaso, P. (2004). Impulsive and compulsive self-injurious behavior and eating disorders: An epidemiological study. In J.L. Levitt, R.A. Sansone & L. Cohn (Eds.) *Self-harm behaviour and eating disorders*. New York, NY: Brunner-Routledge.
Fichter, M.M., Quadflieg, N., Hedlund, S. (2008). Long term course of binge eating disorder and bulimia nervosa: Relevance for nosology and diagnostic criteria. *International Journal of Eating Disorders*, 41, 577–586.
Gibson, P. (2019). *Advances in Effective Brief Psychotherapy*. Carrigtwohill (IE): Lettertec.
Gibson, P., Pietrabissa, G., Manzoni, G.M., Boardman, D., Gori, A., Calstelnuovo, G. (2016). Brief strategic therapy for obsessive-compulsive disorder: A clinical and research protocol of a one-group obeservation study. *BMJ Open*, 6(3), e009118.
Gordon, R.A. (1990). *Anorexia and bulimia: Anatomy of a social epidemic*. Oxford, UK: Basil Blackwell.
Haley, J. (1973). *Uncommon therapy: The psychiatric techniques of MH Erickson*. New York: NY: Norton.
Hay, P., Chinn, D., Forbes, D., Madden, S., Newton, R., Sugenor, L., Touyz, S., Ward, W. (2014). Royal Australian and New Zeland College of Psychiatrists clinical practice guidelines for the treatment of eating disorders. *Australian and New Zealand Journal of Psychiatry*, 48, 11.
Hay, P., McDermott, B. (2009). Individual psychotherapy. In T. Jaffa & B. McDermott (Eds.) *Eating disorders in children and adolescents*. Cambridge, UK: Cambridge University Press.
Jackson, J.B., Pietrabissa, G., Rossi, A., Manzoni, G.M., Castelnuovo, G. (2018). Brief strategic therapy and cognitive behavioral therapy for women with binge eating disorder and comorbid obesity: A randomized clinical trial one-year follow-up. *Journal of Consulting and Clinical Psychology*, 86(8), 688.
Kearns, G., Abdel-Rahaman, S., Alander, S. et al. (2003). Developmental pharmacology-drug disposition, action, and therapy in infants and children. *New England Journal of Medicine*, 349, 1157–1167.
Keys, A., Brozek, J., Henschel, A., Mickelson, O., Taylor, H.L. (1950). *The Biology of Human Starvation* 2 vols. Minneapolis, MN: University of Minnesota Press.
Lacey, J.H., Evans, C.D. (1986). The impulsivity: A multi-impulsive personality disorder. *British Journal of Addiction*, 81(5), 641–649.
Le Grange, D., Lock, J. (2005). The dearth of psychological treatment studies for anorexia nervosa. *International Journal of Eating Disorders*, 37, 79–91.
Le Grange, D. (2016). Elusive etiology of anorexia nervosa: finding answers in an integrative biopsychosocial approach. *Journal of the American Academy of Child & Adolescent Psychiatry*, 1(55), 12–13.
Le Grange, D., Lock, J., Loeb, K. et al. (2010). Academy for Eating Disorders position paper: The role of the family in eating disorders. *International Journal of Eating Disorders*, 43, 1–5.
Le Grange, D. (2004). Family-based treatment vs individual psychotherapy for adolescent bulimia nervosa: What we have learned so far? *Paper presented at the Annual Conference of the Eating Disorders Research Society*. Amsterdam, NL.
Le Grange, D., Lock, J. (2005). The dearth of psychological treatment studies for anorexia nervosa. *International Journal of Eating Disorders*, 37, 79–91.
Le Grange, D., Lock, J., Dymek, M. (2003). Family based therapy for adolescents with bulimia nervosa. *American Journal of Psychotherapy*, 57, 237–251.

Bibliography

Levitt, J., Sansone, R.A., Cohn, L. (2004). *Self-harming behaviour and eating disorders*. New York, NY: Brunner-Routledge.

Lilenfeld, L.R. (2004). Psychiatric comorbidity associated with anorexia nervosa, bulimia nervosa, and binge eating disorder. In T.D. Brewerton (Ed.) *Clinical handbook of eating disorders: An integrated approach*. New York, NY: Marcel Dekker.

Lock, J. (2002). Treating adolescents with eating disorders in the family context. Empirical and theoretical considerations. *Child and Adolescent Psychiatric Clinics of North America*, 11, 331–342.

Lock, J. (2011). Evaluation of family treatment models for eating disorders. *Current Opinion in Psychiatry*, 24, 274–279.

Lock, J., Couturier, J. (2009). Evidence-based family psychotherapy interventions. In T. Jaffa & B. McDermott (Eds.) *Eating disorders in children and adolescents*. Cambridge, UK: Cambridge University Press.

Lock, J., Le Grange, D., Agras, W.S. et al. (2010). Randomized clinical trial comparing family-based treatment with adolescent-focused individual therapy for adolescents with anorexia nervosa. *Archives of General Psychiatry*, 67, 1025–1032.

Loriedo, C. (2013, November 10). Anoressia giovanile, strategie per una terapia efficace ed efficiente. *Seminar presented in Arezzo (Italy)*. Arezzo, IT.

Loriedo, C., Nardone, G., Wazlawick, P., Zeig, Z. (2004). *Strategie e stratagemmi della psicoterapia. Tecniche ipnotiche e non ipnotiche per la soluzione in tempi brevi di problemi complessi*. Milan, IT: FrancoAngeli.

Loriedo, C., Zeig, J., Nardone, G. (2011). *Tranceforming*. Phoenix, AZ: The Milton H. Erickson Foundation Press.

Minuchin, S., Baker, L., Rosman, B.L. et al. (1975). A conceptual model of psychosomatic illness in children. Family organization and family therapy. *Archives of General Psychiatry*, 32, 1031–1038.

Minuchin, S., Rosman, B.L., Baker, L., Minuchin, S. (2009). *Psychosomatic families: Anorexia nervosa in context*. Cambridge, MA: Harvard University Press.

Nardone, G. (1996). *Brief strategic solution-oriented therapy of phobic and obsessive disorders*. Northvale: UK, Jason Aronson.

Nardone, G. (1997). Advanced techniques: From general to specific models of brief therapy. In P. Watzlawick & G. Nardone (Eds.) *Brief strategic therapy*. Lanham, MA: Jason Aronson.

Nardone, G. (1998). *Psicosoluzioni*. Milan, IT: Bur.

Nardone, G. (2003). *Al di là dell'odio e dell'amore per il cibo*. Milan, IT: Bur.

Nardone, G. (2007). *La dieta paradossale*. Milan, IT: Ponte alle Grazie.

Nardone, G. (2009). *Problem solving strategico da tasca*. Milan, IT: Ponte alle Grazie.

Nardone, G. (2016). *La terapia degli attacchi di panico*. Milan, IT: Ponte alle Grazie.

Nardone, G., Balbi, E. (2015). *The logic of therapeutic change: Fitting strategies to pathologies*. London, UK: Karnac.

Nardone, G., Balbi, E., Valteroni, E. (2013). Efficacia ed efficienza della terapia breve strategica nel disturbo ossessivo-compulsivo. In G. Nardone & C. Portelli (Eds.) *Ossessioni compulsioni manie*. Milan, IT: Ponte alle Grazie.

Nardone, G., Barbieri Brook, R. (2010). Advanced brief strategic therapy: An overview of interventions with eating disorders to exemplify how theory and practice work. *European Journal of Psychotherapy and Counselling and Health*, 2(12), 113–127.

Nardone, G., Portelli, C. (2005). *Knowing through changing: The evolution of brief strategic therapy*. Glasgow, UK: Crown House Publishing.

Bibliography 103

Nardone, G., Portelli, C. (2013). *Ossessioni, compulsioni, manie*. Milan, IT: Ponte alle Grazie.

Nardone, G., Rocchi, R., Giannotti, E. (2001). *Modelli di famiglia. Conoscere e risolvere i problemi tra genitori e figli*. Milan, IT: Ponte alle Grazie.

Nardone, G., Salvini, A. (2004). *The strategic dialogue*. London, UK: Karnac.

Nardone, G., Salvini, A. (Eds.) (2019). *International dictionary of psychotherapy*. London, UK: Routledge.

Nardone, G., Selekman, M. (2011). *Uscire dalla trappola. Abbuffarsi, vomitare, torturarsi: La terapia in tempi brevi*. Milan, IT: Ponte alle Grazie.

Nardone, G., Valteroni, E. (2014). *Dieta o non dieta. Per un nuovo equilibrio tra cibo, piacere e salute*. Milan, IT: Ponte alle Grazie.

Nardone, G., Verbitz, T., Milanese, R. (2005). *Prison of food: Research and treatment of eating disorders*. London, UK: Karnac.

Nardone, G., Watzlawick, P. (1993). *The art of change: Strategic therapy and hypnotherapy without trance*. San Francisco, CA: Jossey-Bass.

Nardone, G., Watzlawick, P. (2005). *Brief strategic therapy: Philosophy, techniques and research*. New Jersey: Rowman & Littlefield.

National Collaborating Centre For Mental Health (NCCMH). (2004). *Eating disorders: Core interventions in the treatment and management of anorexia nervosa, bulimia nervosa and related eating disorders. A national clinical practice guideline*. London, UK: National Institute for Clinical Excellence.

Nicholls, D., Bryant-Waugh, R. (2009). Eating disorders of infancy and childhood: Definition, symptomatology, epidemiology, and comorbidity. *Child and Adolescent Psychiatric Clinics*, 18(1), 17–30.

Nielsen, S., Moller-Madsen, S., Isager, T. (1998). Standardized mortality in eating disorders-a quantitative summary of previously published and new evidence. *Journal of Psychosomatic Research*, 44, 412–413.

Petrini, P., Visconti, N., Casadei, A., Mandese, A. (2012). *I disturbi della personalità. Il funzionamento psichico tra normalità e patologia*. Milan, IT: FrancoAngeli.

Pietrabissa, G., Castelnuovo, G., Jackson, J.B., Rossi, A., Manzoni, G.M., Gibson, P. (2019). Brief strategic therapy for bulimia nervosa and binge eating disorder: A clinical and research protocol. *Frontiers in Psychology*, 10, 373.

Robin, A.L., Siegel, P.T., Koepke, T. et al. (1994). Family therapy versus individual therapy for adolescent females with anorexia nervosa. *Journal of Developmental & Behavioral Pediatrics*, 15, 111–116.

Robin, A.L., Siegel, P.T., Moye, A.W. et al. (1999). A controlled comparison of family versus individual therapy for adolescents with anorexia nervosa. *Journal of the American Academy of Child & Adolescent Psychiatry*, 38, 1482–1489.

Robinson, P. (2001). Eating disorders in the UK: Policies for service development and training. *Psychiatric Bulletin*, 25(10), 402.

Royal Australian and New Zeland College of Psychiatrists. (2014). Royal Australian and New Zeland College of Psychiatrists clinical practice guidelines for the treatment of eating disorders. *Australian and New Zeland Journal of Psychiatry*, 48, 977.

Russell, G.F., Szmukler, G.I., Dare, C. et al. (1987). An evaluation of family therapy in anorexia nervosa and bulimia nervosa. *Archives of General Psychiatry*, 44, 1047–1056.

Safer, D.L., Telch, C.F., Chen, E.Y. (2009). *Dialectical behavior therapy for binge eating and bulimia*. New York, NY: Guilford Press.

Selekman, M. (2005). *Pathways to change: Brief therapy with difficult adolescents* (Second edition). New York, NY: Norton.
Selekman, M. (2009). *The adolescent and young adult self-harming treatment manual: A collaborative strengths-based brief therapy approach.* New York, NY: Norton.
Selvini Palazzoli, M. (1963). *L'anoressia mentale.* Milan, IT: Raffaello Cortina.
Steffen, K.J., Roering, J., Mitchell, J.E. (2007). Psychopharmacology and eating disorders. In T. Jaffa & B. McDermott (Eds.) *Eating disorders in children and adolescents.* Cambridge, UK: Cambridge University Press.
Steinhausen, H.C. (2006). Longitudinal perspectives, outcome and prognosis. In T. Jaffa & B. McDermott (Eds.) *Eating disorders in children and adolescents.* Cambridge, UK: Cambridge University Press (2007).
Steinhausen, H.C., Boyadjieva, S., Griogoroiu-Serbanescu, M. et al. (2003). The outcome of adolescent eating disorders: Findings from an international collaborative study. *European Child & Adolescent Psychiatry*, 12(1), 191–198.
Stern, D.N. (2004). *The present moment in psychotherapy and everyday life.* New York, NY: Norton.
Vanderlinden, J. (2001). *Vincere l'anoressia nervosa. Strategie per pazienti, familiari e terapeuti.* Verona: Positive Press.
Waller, G. (1992). Sexual abuse and the severity of bulimic symptoms. *British Journal of Psychiatry*, 161, 90–93.
Waller, G. (2016). Recent advances in psychological therapies for eating disorders. *F1000Research*, 5, F1000 Faculty Rev–702.
Watzlawick, P., Beavin, J.H., Jackson, D.D. (1967). *Pragmatics of human communication: A study of interactional patterns, pathologies and paradoxes.* New York, NY: Norton.
Watzlawick, P., Nardone, G. (2001). *Brief strategic therapy.* London, UK: Karnac.
Wonderlich, S., Myers, T., Norton, M., Crosby, R. (2002). Self-harm and bulimia nervosa: A complex connection. *Eating Disorders*, 10(3), 257–267.
Zerbe, K. (2008). *Integrated treatment of eating disorders.* New York, NY: Norton.

Index

Acquaviva, S. 2
activity 21
ad hoc communication 12
ad hoc therapeutic interventions 8, 41–42
advertising 2–4
affirmation 42–43; *see also* self-image
alcohol 21
Alexander, F. 42
American Psychiatric Association (APA) 1
amphetamines 19–20
anger 21–22
Anorexia Nervosa and Associated Disorders (ANAD) 1
Arezzo Centre, Italy 7, 9, 39, 46–48
armour of anorexia (imprisonment) 8–9, 14, 32, 39
assertive relationships in treatment 41–42
athletic body image 2, 2–4, 7, 33
Saint Augustine 42
Australia (case studies) 45
Austria (case studies) 47–48
autonomy 42–43

Bacon, F. 17–18
balance 14, 16–17, 45–46
Balbi, E. 30
Ball, J. 6, 9, 45, 47
Barbieri Brook, R. 47
beauty: convincing of as treatment 29; ideals 2–4, 7, 33
Belgium (case studies) 47–48
binge eating: breaking patterns 23; bulimia diagnosis 6; clinical classifications 5; early onset/mutation 7–8; effective therapy 44, 45, 47; evocation of sensations 11; polysymptomatic juvenile anorexia 21; therapeutic treatment 32–34;
understanding anorexia 16; unlocking of eating restrictions 12
Biondi, M. 9
black market galenic preparations 20
blaming strategies 32
body image 2–4, 7, 21–22, 29, 33
borderline personality disorder: treatment 39–41; understanding anorexia 20–22
boredom 21–22
brief strategic therapy (BST) 44–45, 48
Bryant-Waugh, R. 8
bulimia nervosa 5, 6–7, 34

Casiero, D. 1
Castelnuovo, G. 7, 47
catabolism 33
"catastrophic" types of therapeutic change 32
Catholic University of Milan 48
chamomile 18–19
chronic symptoms 21–22
clinical classifications 5
clothing 2–3, 13
cognitive behavioural therapy (CBT) 10–11, 33, 47
Colombia (case studies) 47–48
communication: *ad hoc* 12; duels in therapeutic treatments 36; Family Based Treatment 8, 9–10, 13–14, 23–32, 35, 39–41, 45; suggestive-hypnotic 38, 41–42; *see also* Family Based Treatment
comorbid obesity 47
compliance of patients, therapeutic 36
compulsion to vomit *see* vomiting
core muscles 31
Costa, M.B. 46
Couturier, J. 45

Index

daily motor activity in recovery 31–32
Dalle Grave, R. 1, 15, 20, 22, 34–35, 45
Dare, C. 6
death 16–17, 45
"deforming magnifying glass" effect 7
detoxification 30, 39
devaluation of self 21–22
Diagnostic and Statistical Manual of Mental Disorders (DSM) 5, 6, 21
discussion groups 1–2
diuretics 18–19
double bind, therapeutic 24–25
dreaded foods 6–7, 10–11, 17, 24–27, 33, 36, 42
drugs 18–21, 39

early mutation and onset 7–8
effective therapy 44–48
Eisler, I. 6, 45
electrolyte imbalances 16–17
elimination: therapeutic treatment 38–39; understanding anorexia 18–19
Elkaim, M. 5, 6
emotional corrective experiences 42
emotional instability 21–22
empirical studies 6, 8–9, 46
emptiness, feelings of 21–22
emulative suicide 4
enemas 18–19
equilibrium 6; *see also* balance
Europe (case studies) 47–48; Arezzo Centre 7, 9, 39, 46–48; Rome administration 3–4
evocation of sensations 10–11, 38, 42; *see also* pleasure of eating/forbidden foods
evolution for eating disorders 6, 35
excessive motor activity 21
exercising 15–16; breaking patterns 23; clinical classifications 5; effective therapy 45; polysymptomatic juvenile anorexia 21; reframing the responsibility of parents 25; therapeutic treatment 25, 30–32; understanding anorexia 15–16
exotic/eastern eating habits 19
extreme fatigue 14
extremes of idealisation 21–22

Faculty of Psychology of the Catholic University of Milan 48
failure: short of perfection 14; therapeutic 47–48

Family Based Treatment 8, 9–10, 13–14, 23–32, 35, 39–41, 45
Faravelli, C. 20
fashion 2–3, 13
fasting 6–7, 17, 21, 32–34
fatigue 14, 20
Favaro, A. 18
FDA (Food and Drug Administration) 20
fear: of fasting 32–33; of getting fat 34–35; of growing up 42–43; of major weight gain 35; pleasure of eating/forbidden foods 6–7, 10–11, 17, 24–27, 33, 36, 42
"feeling" rather than "understanding" *see* evocation of sensations
Fichter, M.M. 1
fitness trainer skills 31–32
Food and Drug Administration (FDA) 20
forbidden foods 6–7, 10–11, 17, 24–27, 33, 36, 42
force-feeding 11
France (case studies) 47–48

galenic products 19–20
Gibson, P. 7
Goethe, J.W. von 4
group-belonging effect 11–12
growing up, fear of 42–43

Haley, J. 5
Hay, P. 8, 45
hiding food 17
homeostatic eating pathologies 8
hospitalisation 11–12, 45
hunger 19–20, 33

iatrogenic damage 18–19
ICD (International Classification of Diseases) 21
idealisation issues 2–4, 7, 21–22, 33
identity/group-belonging effect 11–12
illusion of alternative 24
imbalances of electrolytes 16–17
imprisonment 8–9, 14, 32, 39
impulsive behavior 17, 21–22; *see also* substance abuse
independence 42–43
indirect encouragement of weight gain 29
induction of muscle mass catabolism 33
inhibition of sexual drive 14
inhibitory processes (substance abuse) 19–20
instability of emotions 21–22

Index

International Classification of Diseases (ICD) 21
International Dictionary of Psychotherapy 44
interpersonal relationships/skills 21–22, 29–30, 36, 41–42, 45–46
interventions see research-interventions
intestinal evacuation 18–19
inverventions (research-interventions) 5–12
investigation of the disorder 24
ipecac syrup 19–20
irreversible health damage 45
Istituto Superiore di Sanità (National Institute of Health) 7–8
Italy (case studies): Arezzo Centre 7, 9, 39, 46–48; Istituto Superiore di Sanità 7–8; Society of Eating Disorders 48; Society of Pediatrics 8

Jackson, J.B. 33, 47

Kearns, G. 45
Keys, A. 22
kleptomania 21

laxatives 15, 18–19, 38
Le Grange, D. 6, 8, 9–10, 45, 46
Levitt, J. 17
Lichtenberg, G. 48
Lilenfeld, L.R. 22
Lock, J. 6, 8, 9, 45
Loriedo, C. 9, 12
loss of control: binge eating 16; forbidden foods 6–7, 10–11, 17, 24–27, 33, 36, 42; substance abuse 20; therapeutic treatment 32–33

McDermott, B. 8
manoeuvres, therapeutic 31
Maudsen Hospital 9–10
medicines: research-interventions 10–11; therapeutic treatment 39; understanding anorexia 19–20
Melnik, T. 46
Mexico (case studies) 47–48
Minuchin, S. 5
Mitchell, J.E. 45
Mitchell, P. 6, 9, 47
models (fashion) 2–3
motor activity in recovery 29, 31–32
mucous membranes 19
multi-symptomatic treatment 20–22, 39–41
muscle mass catabolism 33

National Association of Anorexia Nervosa and Associated Disorders (ANAD) 1
National Collaborating Centre For Mental Health (NCCMH) 6, 20
National Institute of Health 7–8
natural remedies 38
natural sexual drive 14
Netherlands (case studies) 47–48
New Zealand (case studies) 45
Nicholls, D. 8
Nielsen, S. 1
North America (case studies) 47–48
nutrition in recovery 29

obesity 47
oligosymptomatic anorexia 20–21
online discussion groups 1–2
onset of anorexia 7–9

parental roles 9–10
pathological equilibrium 6
pathology of anorexia 8–9, 11–12
perfectionism 14
pleasing function of self-harm 37
pleasure of eating/forbidden foods 6–7, 10–11, 17, 24–27, 33, 36, 42
polysymptomatic juvenile anorexia 20–22, 39–41
Portelli, C. 6, 37, 46
Postgraduate School of Brief Strategic Therapy 46–48
prison metaphors 8–9, 14, 32, 39
Prisons of Food 6
progressive body dysmorphia 14
protection, need for 42–43
protocol, therapeutic 31
psychological balance 45–46
psychopathology 1–4
psychopharmacological treatments 45
psychotropic drugs 20
pure juvenile anorexia 13–14
purging see vomiting
purification of intestines 18–19

Randomised Controlled Trial (RCT) 47
RANZCP (Royal Australian and New Zealand College of Psychiatrists) 45
recovery of nourishment 27
reframing of thought 24–30, 31, 32–33, 36, 38
regaining weight (recovery of nourishment) 27, 29

relapse risk 38–39
relationships *see* interpersonal relationships
relaxation towards pleasant things 36
remission of disorders 6
repulsion for weight loss 7
research-interventions 5–12
restricted anorexia 6–7; polysymptomatic juvenile anorexia 21; therapeutic treatment 32–34; vomiting 17
risk of death 16–17, 45
risk of social situations 13
ritualisation of the ritual 37
Robin, A.L. 6, 9, 45, 47
Robinson, P. 8
Romania (case studies) 47–48
Rome administration 3–4
Royal Australian and New Zealand College of Psychiatrists (RANZCP) 45
runway models 2–3
Russell, G.F. 6, 9, 45
Russia (case studies) 47–48

Saint Augustine 42
Salvini, A. 41–42, 46–47
Scientific Institute for Research, Hospitalization and Healthcare 48
sedative function of self-harm 37
Selekman, M. 7–8, 9; effective therapy 46; polysymptomatic juvenile anorexia 21, 22; self-harming 18; STC 46; vomiting 16–17
self-harming 7–8; breaking patterns 23; polysymptomatic juvenile anorexia 21; therapeutic treatment 37–38; understanding anorexia 18, 21
self-help groups 11–12
self-image problems 2–4, 7, 21–22, 29, 33
self-induced vomiting 16–17
Selvini Palazzoli, M. 5
Service and Laboratory of Clinical Psychology of the IRCCS 48
sexual drive 14; promiscuity 21
ship/captain/helm metaphors in treatment 41–42
SIS-DCA (Italian Society of Eating Disorders) 48
slimness (beauty ideals) 2–4, 7, 33
small, pleasant food transgressions 7, 33
snowball effects 7, 21
social desirability (beauty ideals) 2–4, 7, 33
social dynamics/skills 21–22, 29–30, 36, 41–42, 45–46

social media 35
Society of Eating Disorders 48
Society of Pediatrics 8
South America (case studies) 47–48
Spain (case studies) 47–48
specialised clinics/self-help groups 11–12
staying in shape 31–32, 33
stealing food 17
Steffen, K.J. 20, 45
Steinhausen, H.C. 1
Stern, D.N. 42
strategic blaming 32
Strategic Therapy Centre of Arezzo 9
Strategic Therapy Centre (STC) 7, 9, 39, 46–48
stretching/strengthening exercises for core muscles 31
strongly evocative images 10–11, 24–30, 38, 42
substance abuse: effective therapy 45; polysymptomatic juvenile anorexia 21; therapeutic treatment 39; understanding anorexia 18–21
suggestive-hypnotic communication 38, 41–42
suicide: polysymptomatic anorexia 21; self-harming 18; *Werther effect* 4
swimsuits 13
syrups 19–20
systemic-family therapy 44–45

theft 17
therapeutic compliance of patients 36
therapeutic double bind 24–25
therapeutic innovations 6–7
therapeutic treatment 23–43; binge eating 32–34; borderline personality disorder 39–41; breaking patterns 23–30; CBT 10–11, 33, 47; elimination 38–39; exercising 25, 30–32; self-harming 37–38; summary 41–43; vomiting 25, 32–33, 34–36
topiramate 20
toxins 19, 33
transgressive compulsions 6–7, 10–11, 17, 19, 24–27, 33, 36, 42

understanding anorexia 13–22; binge eating 16; borderline personality disorder 20–22; elimination 18–19; exercising 15–16; polysymptomatic juvenile anorexia 20–22; pure juvenile anorexia

13–14; self-harming 18, 21; substance abuse 18–21; vomiting 16–18
unisex ideals 2
United States (case studies) 47–48

Vanderlinden, J. 6, 10
verbal duels in therapeutic treatments 36
vicious cycle of juvenile anorexia 15–16
victimhood 17
vomiting: breaking patterns 23; bulimia diagnosis 6–7; clinical classifications 5; early onset/mutation 7–8; effective therapy 44, 45; evocation of sensations 11; exercising 15; juvenile anorexia 16–18; polysymptomatic juvenile anorexia 21; reframing the responsibility of parents 25; substance abuse 19–20; therapeutic treatment 25, 32–33, 34–36; understanding anorexia 16–18; unlocking of eating restrictions 12

Waller, G. 17, 46
water-based enemas 18–19
Watzlawick, P. 5, 6, 7, 41–42, 46
Werther effect 4
World Health Organization (WHO) 1

Zerbe, K. 17

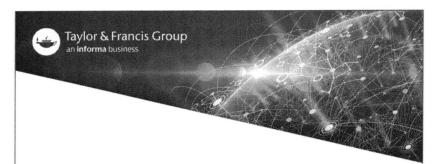